SUNDAY HOMILIES

Saint Vincent Archabbey
Cycle C

Demetrius R. Dumm, O.S.B.
Campion P. Gavaler, O.S.B.

ARCHABBEY PUBLICATIONS
2015

ARCHABBEY PUBLICATIONS
300 Fraser Purchase Road,
Latrobe, Pennsylvania 15650-2690
www.stvincentstore.com

Library of Congress Cataloging-in-Publication Data

Dumm, Demetrius, 1923-2013
Sunday homilies : Saint Vincent Archabbey / Demetrius R. Dumm, O.S.B., Campion P. Gavaler, O.S.B.—1 [edition].
volumes cm
Includes bibliographical references and index.
Contents:—Cycle C.
ISBN 978-0-9906855-1-7 (v. 3)
1. Bible. Gospels--Sermons. 2. Church year sermons. 3. Common lectionary (1992) 4. Saint Vincent Archabbey (Latrobe, Pa.)--Sermons. 5. Catholic Church--Sermons. I. Gavaler, Campion P. II. Title.
BS2555.54.D86 2014
252'.6--dc23

2014031583

Printed in the United States of America

Cover photo:
Mosaic of a winged ox as symbol of Saint Luke the Evangelist in Iglesia de San Manuel y San Benito, Madrid, by architect Fernando Arbos, 19th century. Used with permission.

Archabbey Publications editorial team:
Kimberley Opatka-Metzgar, Director;
Rev. Aaron Buzzelli, O.S.B., Elizabeth Cousins, Jordan Hainsey,
Miranda Senchur, Simon Stuchlik and Alexis Zawelensky.
Cover design: Jordan Hainsey.

Additional Permissions

Dedicated to
Archabbot Douglas R. Nowicki, O.S.B.

Contents

Foreword

Pope Francis has given us a kind of humorous, non-scientific test to discern whether or not the purpose of a Sunday Mass has been realized. Its purpose has been realized if the people leaving church after Mass will look like people who have just heard good news. Perhaps Pope Francis had this simple test in mind when he gave the title "The Joy of the Gospel" to his apostolic exhortation in which he stresses the importance of the homily in announcing good news.

Many priests, religious and lay persons have told me that Father Demetrius and Father Campion in their interpretations of the Sunday gospels have helped them realize that each gospel is, in fact, good news. It is always good news to hear with deeper understanding that the Risen Lord is with us, loving us in all the circumstances of our lives.

It is my hope that the Archabbey's publication of these "Sunday Homilies" by Father Demetrius and Father Campion in book form will help many more people to act, to speak, and to look like people who have heard and who believe the good news of the gospel.

+ Douglas R. Nowicki, O.S.B.

Archabbot Douglas Nowicki, O.S.B.

Advent Season

First Sunday of Advent
Luke 21:25-28, 34-36

Gospel Summary

Luke places Jesus' discourse about the destruction of the temple and his coming at the end of the world immediately before the narrative of his death and resurrection. In the present passage Jesus uses cosmic symbolic images of the prophetic tradition to indicate the final divine action in history at the end of the world. Before the Son of Man comes in a cloud with power and glory, there will be signs in the sun, the moon, and the stars. The coming of the Son of Man in power and glory means that the final redemption is at hand. Jesus then issues a warning lest our hearts become drowsy from carousing and drunkenness or from anxieties of daily life. If we are not vigilant, the final day will catch us by surprise like a trap. Jesus tells us to pray for the strength to escape the ever-imminent tribulation so that we may stand erect with raised heads at his coming.

Life Implications

The gospel passage addresses the terrifying experience of one's world coming to an end—not only the final end of world, but also of our individual worlds such as our financial security, our marriage, our health, our life in dying. These are terrifying experiences not only because of the physical suffering they may entail, but because the tribulation may lead to despair about the meaning of life itself.

Friedrich Nietzsche (d. 1900) anticipated that total loss of meaning which now seems to be so pervasive in our culture when he proclaimed: "God is dead...Do we not wander through an endless nothingness?" Ernest Hemingway (d. 1961) in one of his short stories has a character express the despair of the loss of meaning in a prayer without meaning: "Our nada (Spanish word for 'nothing') who art in nada, nada be thy name..." and "Hail Nothing, full of nothing, nothing is with thee..." Steven

Weinberg, a 1979 Nobel Prize winner for physics, writes: "...this present universe has evolved from an unspeakably unfamiliar early condition, and faces a future extinction of endless cold or intolerable heat. The more the universe seems comprehensible the more it also seems pointless" (*The First Three Minutes*).

Jesus, too, had the experience of his own world coming to an end—his arrest, suffering and death were imminent. He, however, had the courage to face the loss of his life in hope because he trusted that God would not abandon his beloved Son to the meaningless nothing of death. Jesus, identifying himself with all creation as God's dwelling place, realized that with his death would also come the end of the temple and the world. In the biblical tradition temple and the universe were inseparably joined. God created the universe as a temple for his children to enjoy and for worship on the seventh day. In turn, the temple was the universe in miniature also created for Sabbath worship and joy. We fallen creatures, however, had turned his Father's house of prayer --the temple and the universe—into a den of thieves.

The old creation of temple and world in a sense would already come to an end with the death of Jesus. The Romans in response to a Jewish revolt in fact destroyed Jerusalem and the temple in the year 70. The end, however, in the mystery of God's creative love would at the same time be the beginning of a new creation—first in the resurrection of Jesus, and then in the creation of a new spiritual temple, a New Jerusalem, a new heaven, and a new earth (Rev 21).

Advent is a time of vigilance and prayer. We ask for the gift of sharing the hope and courage of Christ so that we can with his trust face the terrifying experience of our own world falling apart. Jesus is the leader and perfector of our faith. Following him, for the sake of the joy that is before us, we will endure the cross, despising its shame (Heb 12:2). The universe and our human existence in it are not pointless. We do not wander through an endless nothingness. Advent is also a celebration of the good news that the Risen Lord comes to be with us now—in the Eucharist, in the words of Scripture, in the Church, in the least of our brothers and sisters, in all our joys and sorrows. We will stand erect with raised heads at his coming because our redemption is at hand. " 'Yes, I am coming soon.' Amen! Come, Lord Jesus!" (Rev 22:20).

Campion P. Gavaler, O.S.B.

Second Sunday of Advent
Luke 3:1-6

Gospel Summary

Luke's elaborate attempt to locate the arrival of John the Baptist in the context of secular history seems to be the answer to every historian's prayer. In fact, however, these references are very imprecise, and none more so than the apparently decisive "fifteenth year of the reign of Tiberius Caesar." The problem is that the Roman emperor Tiberius shared power with Augustus for two years and we do not know when Luke is beginning his count of the years of Tiberius' reign. One must wonder whether Luke is not perhaps smiling to himself as he teases historians in this way.

Be that as it may, there is no doubt that Luke is very much interested in history. But it is a history that includes God's intervention to bring final salvation from the human scourge of sin and death. This divine "taking charge" of history will be announced by John the Baptist and brought into being by Jesus. However, only those who are ready to embrace God's gracious purposes will participate in the final victory.

John's "baptism of repentance" is a ritual that signifies one's readiness to remove all obstacles to the coming of the Lord. Such obstacles would be, first and foremost, a prideful self-will that wishes to dictate where and how and when the Lord should come. Making straight the way of Lord is, therefore, a metaphor for personal conversion from prideful controlling tendencies to humble and grateful acceptance of God's sovereign rights in human life.

Life Implications

The most certain way to miss the promised "salvation of God" is to be too busy, too engrossed in one's work and too distracted to think about God or to prepare for his coming. It is true, of course, that Christ came some 2000 years ago. But that is no guarantee that we have welcomed him. For Christ continues to come to each generation of us humans and to challenge us to let his ideals govern our lives. In that sense, God is always coming and we are constantly being asked to welcome him.

This does not mean that we need to devote large amounts of time to welcoming Christ into our lives. It is more a matter of quality than of quantity. The ideal is set forth in the famous "Hear, O Israel," of Deuteronomy 6:4. We are told there that we should never be totally unmindful of the reality and the presence of God in our lives. In time of explicit prayer, God is at center stage, as it were, while at other times he moves into the wings but never far from full consciousness on our part.

I like to think of this consciousness of God's presence as a "benign distraction" which, far from interfering with our work, actually helps us to focus more clearly on what we are doing. Moreover, it should not be surprising, when we think of God's love for us, that a smile should play occasionally across our faces, as is customary with those who are in love. Such a benign distraction not only makes us more productive but it also gives us a deep sense of peace and security.

It is our recognition of the presence of God in our world, whether in the fifteenth year of Tiberius Caesar, or in December 2012, as this is written, that constitutes the true meaning of history for us.

Demetrius R. Dumm, O.S.B.

Third Sunday of Advent
Luke 3:10-18

Gospel Summary

Immediately preceding this passage, Luke tells us that the word of God had come upon John the Baptist in the desert. John then began to proclaim the coming of the Lord: all flesh would at last see the salvation of God. John also proclaimed the necessity of turning from evil in repentance in order to prepare for the Lord's coming.

The crowds ask, "What then should we do?" John replies that whoever has two cloaks or food should share with the person who has none. Tax collectors should not collect more than what is prescribed. Soldiers should not practice extortion or falsely accuse anyone, and they should be satisfied with their wages. The people are filled with expectation, wondering whether John might be the Messiah. John responds that one mightier than he will come, and will baptize with the Holy Spirit and fire. John warns that when the Messiah comes, he will gather the wheat into his barn, and burn the chaff with unquenchable fire.

Life Implications

We will celebrate with gratitude the Lord's coming among us in the past on Christmas. Advent, however, is a time to affirm our faith that the Lord's coming is also a present and future reality for which we must prepare. We too ask, "Teacher, what should we do?" The ordinary-ness of John's reply to our question is surprising: share what you have with those who have nothing; do your job without cheating or telling lies; be satisfied with what you earn.

Someone asked Saint Philip Neri (who happened to be playing cards at the time) what he would do if he learned that his death was imminent. Philip Neri replied that he would continue playing cards. The best preparation for the Lord's coming at any moment is to be doing what we ought to be doing. In the words of the old Shaker hymn: "'Tis a gift to be simple, 'Tis a gift to be free, 'Tis a gift to come down where we ought to be."

There is also a surprising ordinary-ness about the Lord's coming—the divine presence does not force itself upon us with bells and whistles. When Jesus did come as Messiah, most people did not recognize him because he did not meet their expectations. Would God allow the Messiah to be defeated and disgraced by dying on a cross like a criminal? Advent thus is also a season to ask for the grace to be freed from false expectations about the Lord's coming into our lives.

Perhaps the most ordinary and most surprising way of all that the Lord comes to us is in the reality of the Present Moment. Each moment becomes a sacrament of divine presence if we say in faith, "It is the Lord." It is thus possible to bless the Lord at all times because every moment without exception is a grace of divine, self-giving love to us. The Lord is with us even in those tragic moments beyond understanding that seem to be without meaning. Life either has no meaning at all, or has total meaning because the Lord is present in all its moments.

Saint Paul tells us the wonderful life-implications of trust in the Lord's presence at every moment in all the circumstance of our lives: "Rejoice always. Pray without ceasing. In all circumstances give thanks...Have no anxiety at all...Then the peace of God that surpasses all understanding will guard your hearts and minds in Christ Jesus" (1 Thes 5:16-18 and Phil 4:6-7).

Campion P. Gavaler, O.S.B.

Fourth Sunday of Advent
Luke 1:39-45

Gospel Summary

On the carefully programmed Advent journey to Christmas, the Fourth Sunday belongs to Mary. This is so because Christmas, which celebrates the birth of Jesus, necessarily involves the motherhood of Mary. However, the story of that birth is reserved for Midnight Mass, while today's gospel tells us how Mary prepared for that wonderful event by accepting the message of an angel, which meant allowing God to determine how she could be a mother and remain a virgin.

If through the centuries Mary has captured the imagination of the Catholic world, it is in large measure because she faced the mystery of God and said, "May it be done to me according to your word." (1:38) Even her greatest privilege as mother of the Savior presupposes this radical trust and generosity on her part.

It is easy to ignore the mystery of God until the very end of life. It is also easy to live in fear of that mystery. However, human life will never be really successful until we learn to embrace God's mystery with trust and confidence. Mary shows us how to do that and what wonderful results will follow.

Life Implications

Although we know very little about the "historical" Mary, her symbolic presence is real and powerful. In her case, symbolic truth presupposes an historical person but it reveals the universal and perennial significance of that person. It is a truth that transcends such limitations as age, race and gender as it reveals the meaning of Mary, Virgin and Mother, for all human beings everywhere.

As a virgin, Mary represents hope. Indeed, there are few images that capture the meaning of hope and promise more effectively than that of a youthful young lady. All of us, then, who strive to be positive and joyful and hopeful in a weary and despairing society, can look to virginal Mary as a model who is ready and willing to inspire and encourage us. As a mother, and specifically as the mother of our Savior, Mary is also the most perfect model of fruitfulness. She represents, therefore, both virginal, promising springtime and fruitful, bountiful summer. She conquers cold, barren winter in our hearts and leads us to a rich and meaningful harvest.

There is such a temptation to live off of others and to complain rather than to contribute. Constant griping and blaming others means an empty harvest. By contrast, Mary models for us a life that is wonderfully fruitful through loving concern for the welfare and happiness of others. There is no better way to prepare for and to celebrate the birth of Jesus!

Demetrius R. Dumm, O.S.B.

Christmas Season

Christmas
Luke 2: 1-14

Gospel Summary

In the gospel passage for Mass at midnight we hear the Christmas story from the Gospel of Luke. It is a story of faith so simple that even a child can grasp it. Yet, even after 2000 years, it is a mystery so profound that the richness of its meaning remains inexhaustible. We are reminded again of God's providential care that makes all history sacred history. The powerful rulers of the world, whether an Egyptian pharaoh or a Roman emperor, may have their armies and issue their decrees, but through the odd coincidences of history, God's own purposes are ultimately achieved. As foretold by the prophet, Mary gives birth to a savior, who is Christ and Lord, in Bethlehem, the city of David.

Caesar Augustus, regarded by Romans as a god who would bring peace and salvation to the world, is now only an unwitting instrument in the divine plan to bring God's peace and salvation through this child born of a young Jewish woman. Mary is the faithful, willing agent of God's loving purpose. After giving birth to her son, with love she wraps him in swaddling clothes and lays him in a manger.

In the gospel passage for Mass at dawn (Lk 2:15-20), Luke continues the love story of Christmas. Now Mary and Joseph share the divine gift of love that they have received by welcoming shepherds—like tax collectors and prostitutes, members of a despised class in their society. The shepherds, like us who also have heard the good news, are now able to sing a new carol with the angels of the heavenly liturgy, glorifying and praising God for the gift of Jesus' presence among us.

The meaning of Luke's Christmas story is completed by the prologue of John's gospel, the passage for Mass during the day (Jn 1:1-18). Christ is born of Mary so that he might be born and live in us. Those who accept the Word-become-flesh through faith become children of God, not by natural generation, but as a divine gift. The meaning of Christmas and God's loving purpose will not be completely realized until the eternal fulfillment of Jesus' Last Supper prayer: "I pray...that they may all be one, as you, Father, are in me and I in you, that they also may be in us..." (Jn 17:20-21).

Life Implications

Despite laments about the commercialism of the Christmas season, the universal instinct of people is correct: at the heart of the mystery of Christmas is giving and receiving gifts. We sense there is more to life than paying a wage or earning a wage. A gift is always a surprise and a joy because as a present of love, it is unearned. Our hearts indeed are restless until we receive love and give love. A gift is the sacramental, symbolic presence of a person. If my gift of love is accepted, it is I who am accepted; if my gift of love is rejected, it is I who am rejected.

One of the surprises of God's self-giving to us is that it seems to be so ordinary, and thus can easily be overlooked. The Word that is God's self-giving to us was to be found not in a royal palace, but in a manger as a helpless baby in need of a mother's love. Today at our Christ-Mass the Risen Lord gives himself to us as bread and wine. What could be more ordinary, and at the same moment so extraordinary a gift of love? It is through the most simple, ordinary means and in the most humble places that of the gift of love can be exchanged.

I am aware that at least one prison chaplain will be using these reflections to prepare his Christmas homily for those in our society who truly are the least of the brothers and sisters of Jesus. They too must hear the good news that no one has the power to take away our worth and dignity because our worth and our dignity are a gift of God's love for us. Those who are not able to buy expensive things—prisoners, the sick, the poor. children—remind us that what truly matters is the gift of our loving presence, however ordinary the means of its incarnation. We do have to become gifts of bread and wine for each other because the Lord loves us and becomes bread and wine for us.

Campion P. Gavaler, O.S.B.

Feast of the Holy Family
Luke 2:41-52

Gospel Summary

At the end of Luke's Infancy Narrative, we find a story that does not really pertain to his infancy, since he is already twelve years old when he visits the temple with his parents on the occasion of the Passover feast. He is there because he has now reached the age of "maturity" and must therefore join the pilgrimage to Jerusalem for the major feasts.

We must be careful not to be distracted by paintings of this scene of Jesus with the doctors of the law. In such cases, he is often pictured standing in the center of a circle of old men, with a halo on his head, and in a pose of one who is teaching. In the text, however, we read that he was "sitting in the midst of the teachers, listening to them and asking them questions." This would be the normal situation of a bright and curious young person. There does seem to be some form of dialogue also, for the old men are "astounded at his understanding and his answers."

In the context of Luke's gospel, where choice of vocation is of paramount importance, Jesus is here presented as one who is beginning to take charge of his life, which means that he is also beginning to establish his independence from parental guidance. Nonetheless, it is important to note that, at the end of this episode, Jesus returned to Nazareth with his parents and "was obedient to them." This tension between parental control and personal freedom makes this an especially appropriate gospel for the feast of the Holy Family.

Life Implications

There is much in this gospel that is important for the delicate and critical task of responsible parenting. As teen-age children begin to test the boundaries of their lives, parents are faced with the enormous responsibility of steering a middle course between a rigid and authoritarian solution and a lax and indulgent attitude. The authoritarian model prevents a child from developing in a normal and healthy way and can lead to later demands for freedom that are bitter and sometimes violent. But lax indulgence is no good solution either, for it allows children to make decisions, and face consequences, for which they are not prepared. Granting too much freedom too soon can look like love, but it may be simply a form of abandonment.

I have never had to face the difficult problem of parenting, but I did have an analogous experience when I was rector of our seminary for seventeen years in the days of Vatican II. We all knew that the rigid regime that had prevailed in seminaries would have to be changed, but of course the students had a much more radical change in mind than the rector! The boundaries needed to be moved, but the desire of some students was to have no boundaries at all. I soon learned that governing by fiat would not work...and so we had endless discussion about what a reasonable compromise would be. In such circumstances, what is at issue is the concern one has for the long-term benefit of the students rather than for good order alone.

I think a parallel situation for parents would be the perennial struggle that occurs when a teenager is trying to choose a good college. It is not a very good idea to make that critical choice simply on the basis of where this teenager's boy friend or girl friend is going to college! This is especially true when we realize that this boy friend or girl friend will probably not turn out to be one's marriage partner after all. But this is only one of many choices where parents and children must dialogue with sincerity and trust. And the critical ingredient is a tough love that is in touch with reality and which engenders real trust.

In terms of today's gospel, we note that Jesus asserted his independence from parental constraints but nonetheless returned with them to Nazareth and "was obedient to them." I think it is safe to say that his career was not endangered by such a wise sense of balance.

Demetrius R. Dumm, O.S.B.

Epiphany
Matthew 2:1-12

Gospel Summary

The Epiphany gospel is a continuation of the Christmas story in Matthew's prologue to his gospel (chapters 1-2). The prologue is a theological masterpiece in narrative form through which Matthew anticipates the major historical events he will present in his gospel to explain the significance of Jesus for us.

The names of Jesus are revealed: Messiah, King, Son of David, Son of Abraham, Emmanuel (God with us). As Son of Abraham, Jesus fulfills the divine promise that in Abraham's seed "all the nations of the earth will find blessing" (Gn 22:18). The miracle of the virginal conception heralds the beginning of the climactic end-time of sacred history. The gentile nations as foretold by the prophet Isaiah come to the New Zion with their treasures to praise the Lord. Jesus will be rejected by many, will suffer persecution and death, but will ultimately triumph through the Father's providential care in the resurrection.

In today's gospel reading, Matthew tells us that when Jesus was born in Bethlehem, magi from the East arrived in Jerusalem looking for the newborn king of the Jews. When King Herod heard this, he was troubled, and asked the magi to bring him word of the child's whereabouts so that he too could honor him. When the magi found the child with Mary, his mother, they offered their gifts in homage. Warned in a dream not to return to King Herod, they departed for their own country by another way.

Life Implications

The good news of Epiphany is that Jesus reveals the mystery of God to be self-giving love. Jesus is the epiphany of the invisible God in all the events of his life: as a helpless child lying in a manger, as a young man dying on a cross--the ultimate revelation that God's glory is love. This feast reminds us that each Sunday's liturgy with its gospel reading is an epiphany of the Lord to be reflected upon in prayerful study.

As in every offering of love, the Lord awaits the response of our hearts. Will it be that of King Herod who perceives it as a threat to his own autonomy and power? Will it be that of the magi who perceive the Lord's offering of love as the fulfillment of the human quest for the ultimate meaning of life? Christina Rossetti in her lovely Epiphany poem "In the Bleak Mid-Winter" shows us the response that brings joy to the sacred heart of Jesus:

> "What can I give him poor as I am?
> If I were a shepherd I would bring a lamb
> If I were a wise man I would do my part
> Yet what I can I give him Give my heart."

The meaning of Epiphany would be incomplete if we focus our attention solely upon God's self-revelation in the past as described in Sacred Scripture. God's Epiphany is a present event—in the wonders of the universe and nature; in the events of our personal history and world history; in the works of science and technology, music, art and architecture; in the sacraments; in people. In our liturgy today we pray for the vision to recognize God's epiphanies, and the grace to extend a grateful welcome.

Every person is also called upon to be an Epiphany of God just as Jesus in his humanity was an Epiphany of the divine mystery. Every person in the unique particularity of his or her life can reveal an aspect of God's truth, goodness and beauty that otherwise would forever remain unknown. Today we also pray for the grace to be totally transparent so that God's glory may be made visible through us, and that people might discover peace and joy in that glory.

Campion P. Gavaler, O.S.B.

Lenten Season

First Sunday of Lent
Luke 4:1-13

Gospel Summary

Filled with the Holy Spirit, Jesus is led by the Spirit into the desert to be tempted by the devil. Recall that this event comes immediately after Jesus' baptism in the Jordan. After his baptism Jesus was praying when the Holy Spirit descended upon him, and a voice came from heaven saying, "You are my beloved Son." (3: 22) The devil now says to Jesus, "If you are Son of God, command this stone to become bread." Then the devil promises all of the kingdoms of the world if Jesus would worship him. Finally the devil challenges Jesus to throw himself from the parapet of the temple to prove that since he is God's Son, he would not be injured. Jesus triumphs over each temptation.

Life Implications

The writers of the gospels clearly affirm the humanity of Jesus. However, it is unlikely that they would have dared to say that Jesus was tempted by the devil--with the implication of the possibility of failure--unless Jesus himself had spoken of the trials he was undergoing. The Letter to the Hebrews expresses the tradition that Jesus initiated: "For we do not have a high priest who is unable to sympathize with our weaknesses, but one who has similarly been tested in every way, yet without sin." (4:15) In the dramatic confrontation between the devil and Jesus, Luke indicates that until the day Jesus died, the devil attempted to entice him from fidelity to his Father's will and to his mission.

Luke explains the meaning of the temptations Jesus underwent by using the Book of Deuteronomy description of the temptations that Israel underwent in the desert wilderness. The key to interpretation lies in the text known in Hebrew as the Shema: "Hear, O Israel! The Lord is our God, the Lord alone. Therefore, you shall love the Lord, your God, with your whole heart, and with all your whole being, and with your whole strength." (Dt 6: 4-5) The Dominican bible scholar Jerome Murphy-O'Connor explains how the Shema was understood in Jesus' time (*Bible Review,* August 1999).

"With your whole heart" means with a heart undivided by a contrary desire. In the desert wilderness the people's craving for food divided their hearts from trust in God's care for them. Jesus, however, would not allow his craving for food to divide his heart from complete trust in his Father's care. "With your whole soul" means trust in God even if you should lose your life. In the wilderness the people were afraid they were going to die of thirst, and demanded evidence of God's presence: "The Israelites quarreled there and tested the Lord, saying 'Is the Lord in our midst or not?'"(Ex 17:7). Jesus, however, would not ask God to prove his presence by saving him if he jumped off the temple parapet. (Luke places this temptation last in his sequence because his whole gospel is a narrative of Jesus' journey to Jerusalem. There he will choose fidelity to his Father's will and mission over the desire to save his own life.) "With your whole strength" means with all your wealth. After the Israelites reached the Promised Land, they are warned that their wealth would cause them to forget the Lord, and to worship false gods and demons. The devil, understanding the allure of wealth, promises to give Jesus all the kingdoms of the world if he would forget God, and worship him. Jesus said to the devil in reply, "It is written: 'You shall worship the Lord, your God, and him alone shall you serve'" (4: 8).

The temptations of Jesus point back to the temptations of Israel in the past, and point forward to the trials that the Church in all its members will undergo in the future. It is now we who are in the wilderness, with no lasting city, on a journey to the Promised Land. Each trial that life brings even to our dying day is a crisis, but is also an opportunity to trust more completely that the Lord is with us, and that we do love God with all our heart, and with all our soul, and with all our might. We are confident that we will triumph in our trials of faith, not because of our own strength, but because Jesus has given us his holy Spirit. Thus sharing the fidelity of his undivided heart, we can pray with confidence: Our Father, do not let us be defeated by temptation, but deliver us from the evil one.

Campion P. Gavaler, O.S.B.

Second Sunday of Lent
Luke 9:28b-36

Gospel Summary

Luke's version of the transfiguration of Jesus is more personal than the accounts of Mark and Matthew. Thus, for example, Luke alone tells us that Jesus was at prayer when this occurred. And he alone informs us concerning the subject of Jesus' conversation with Moses and Elijah, that they "spoke of his exodus that he was going to accomplish in Jerusalem" (9: 31).

Moses and Elijah represent the Old Testament which is centered in the exodus of God's people from the bondage of Egypt. Correspondingly, the exodus of Jesus in Jerusalem, which is his death and resurrection, will be a new exodus initiating a new covenant between God and all the people of the world. This new exodus must happen on the anniversary of the exodus from Egypt and will be the fulfillment of that pivotal event.

The liberation of the Hebrew slaves from the bondage of the Pharoah was the effect of a divine initiative revealing God's true nature as one who loves and who wishes that all in bondage should be free. This same revelation is at the center of the definitive exodus, which is the death and resurrection of Jesus. Moreover, just as the Passover meal in Israel kept alive the power of the original exodus, so also does the Eucharist of Christians make present among us the love of God as one who offers true and lasting freedom.

Life Implications

The luminous aura that surrounded Jesus on that mountaintop was an external manifestation of his ecstatic recognition that God's plan of salvation—God's ultimate exodus—will be brought about by his own loving sacrifice. His loving vulnerability thus becomes the surprising vehicle for God's power to save the world. In effect, loving concern for others is revealed as the only power with beneficent and lasting results.

This kind of loving vulnerability does not mean that we are called to be passive or compliant. In fact, this kind of loving is persistent and relentless at the same time that it is gracious and sensitive. For it results from a passionate commitment to the ideal of love received and then offered to others. The only true source of freedom is unselfish love, and the only valid purpose of such freedom is to enable one to love others so that they also may be free.

This equation is clearly implied in the command of God to Israel in Deuteronomy 24:17, where the now liberated Israelites are told to care for the vulnerable ones, for example, the widow, the orphan and the wayfarer. They must do so simply because they were once themselves desperately weak and vulnerable and God loved them into freedom and self-confidence.

The transfigured Jesus represents the full awareness of this incredible wisdom of God. And when the voice from heaven commands us to "listen to him" (9: 35), we are challenged to be transfigured by our own recognition of this wisdom as we become more and more ready to use our freedom so that others also may be free—free from fear and guilt and poverty and pain.

Demetrius R. Dumm, O.S.B.

Third Sunday of Lent
Luke 13:1-9

Gospel Summary

The gospel passage refers to two recent tragedies that were on people's minds. Pilate had ordered the massacre of some Galileans who had come to Jerusalem to offer sacrifices in the temple. And eighteen people had been killed when a tower at Siloam fell on them. Jesus comments that the victims of these tragedies were no greater sinners than other people were. He then says: "But I tell you, if you do not repent, you will all perish as they did!" Then he tells them the parable about the person who had planted a fig tree that did not bear any fruit. When the owner ordered it to be cut down, the gardener asked for another year of cultivation to see if the fig tree would finally bear fruit before it was cut down.

Life Implications

Jesus uses the experiences of the worst possible human tragedies in order to reveal the possibility of even a greater spiritual tragedy. We are all in a state not only of physical death, but of spiritual death as well. Unless we turn to God to be saved from our condition of spiritual death, Jesus warns us, all of us will remain in it and perish. Saint Paul particularly in his Letter to the Romans clearly spells out the reality of the death-culture to which Jesus alludes: "Jews and Greeks alike that they are all under the domination of sin" (3:9). And this condition of Sin (alienation from God, the source of life) Paul equates with Death.

The human condition of Sin/Death, initiated by the first humans, pre-exists the sins of individuals and is not their responsibility, even though they have added to it by their own personal sins. Without God's liberating grace, human beings would remain helplessly mired in a state of enslavement to Sin/Death. Jesus says: Realize the truth of the state you are in. Accept the liberated life of God's kingdom that I now offer you, or you will all perish. It is easy to see why Jesus is distressed by the illusion of self-righteousness that makes repentance and liberation from Sin/Death impossible. I can think of no better illustrations of this most fundamental teaching of Jesus than the fiction of Flannery O'Connor. Her short stories have the power to awaken us to the truth that we are all inextricably involved in evil, and are all in dire need of God's liberating, saving grace.

After the warning about perishing in our sinful state unless we repent, Luke adds Jesus' parable about the fig tree. We may be liberated from our fallen state of Sin/Death and stand in freedom like a fig tree. However, if we choose evil and do not bear the fruit of good work, we will be cut down like a useless fig tree. In the second reading of today's Mass (1 Cor 10:1-6, 10-12), Paul forcefully emphasizes the warning of Jesus' parable. Paul writes that his ancestors were liberated for new life with God from their condition of death-slavery in Egypt. However, under pressure of their trials they succumbed to evil desires and thus reverted to a state of enslavement. "God was not pleased with most of them, for they were struck down in the desert."

The experience of the liberated slaves in the desert, Paul tells us, is meant to serve as an example for us so that we will not desire evil things. If we do, we would revert to our original enslavement to Sin/Death as idolaters, seeking life where it cannot be found. Paul's warning is an apt comment on the teaching of Jesus' parable: "Therefore whoever thinks he is standing secure should take care not to fall." At the same time, in the Spirit of Jesus, he offers us a word of comfort: "God is faithful and will not let you be tried beyond your strength; but with the trial he will also provide a way out, so that you may be able to bear it" (1 Cor 10: 12-13).

Campion P. Gavaler, O.S.B.

Fourth Sunday of Lent
Luke 15:1-3.11-32

Gospel Summary

When we read the parables of Jesus, we need to remind ourselves that they are not accounts of historical events. Rather, they are stories with a spiritual lesson for all times and places. In most cases, these stories are not new to the audience. They are really old, familiar stories, which are much appreciated when they are told well. Jesus tells the stories very well indeed but he also adds a "twist" to the narrative. By telling the story so well he captivates his audience and then, once they are drawn into the story, he surprises them with a spiritual application.

The story in today's gospel about a father and his two sons is an old story, going back at least as far as Esau and Jacob. In this story, the elder son is very dutiful but also rather dull. The younger son, by contrast, is wild and unpredictable but also interesting and attractive. In the classic story, the younger son sows his wild oats but then repents and is welcomed home with joy. The older son resents his father's celebration of his brother's salvation and is rejected. The audience is convinced that justice has been done.

In Luke's parable, however, the focus of attention is on the father and especially on his reaction to the elder son's anger. The twist that Jesus adds to the story is the refusal of the father to reject his elder son who in fact is treated by his father with surprising gentleness. When the audience asked why the story had been changed, as we can assume they did, the reply would be that the father is in reality God, who loves his dull and dutiful children just as much as those who are wild and perhaps a bit more interesting.

Life Implications

The wisdom expressed in this parable teaches us that human sin can take the form of wild and rebellious behavior or, perhaps more commonly, of sullen, angry and judgmental attitudes. The civil law is concerned almost exclusively with rebellious behavior but, in the parable, it is clear that the sinfulness of the elder son is much more dangerous.

Those of us who lead quiet and "responsible" lives may very well fall into the trap of sullen, resentful and angry attitudes toward others who seem to be "getting away with murder." What we need to ask ourselves is whether we have the kind of love that can understand why others, often less privileged than ourselves, may need both correction and forgiveness.

When the elder son in the parable says to his father, "your son," (and, by implication, no brother of mine) has done wrong and should be punished, the father gently corrects him with the words, "Your brother" (and not just my son) "was dead and has come to life again." This wayward son has indeed sinned but he has also repented and has paid a price for his sin. Now it is time to rejoice.

The clear point is that we dare not ever disown our brothers and sisters, who are all children of God. On the contrary, we must love them and rejoice to see them have a chance to repent and be brought back to life again. And this is true of all sorts of people, including both the village prankster and the person on death row. We may feel that some people do not deserve a second chance but the danger of such a judgment is underscored in the challenging words of Jesus that "the measure with which you measure will be measured out to you." (Matt 7:2)

Demetrius R. Dumm, O.S.B.

Fifth Sunday of Lent
John 8:1-11

Gospel Summary

This is the gospel about the woman who had been caught in adultery. Enemies of Jesus bring her to him at daybreak while he is teaching people in the temple area. They make her stand there humiliated in public. In an attempt to trap him into opposing either Mosaic Law or Roman Law, they ask Jesus whether he judges that she should be stoned. After Jesus exposes their malice, the woman's accusers are afraid to condemn her. Beginning with the elders, they all go away. Then Jesus says to the woman: "Neither do I condemn you. Go, [and] from now on do not sin any more."

Life Implications

The story about Jesus and the woman caught in adultery happily became part of Holy Scripture, inserted as it was in the fourth gospel. Some early manuscripts have the story placed after Luke 21:38 where it says that people came at daybreak to listen to Jesus as he taught in the temple area. The story fits very well in the fourth gospel because it illustrates some of its most basic themes–truth, judgment, blindness, sight, darkness, light, death, life, sin, creation.

In Jesus' time it was important to determine the arrival of daybreak when the first offerings were to be made in the temple. A rabbi asked his students what criterion might be used to determine that the night had ended. One student said the night had ended when there was enough light to tell a goat from a sheep. Another said when you could distinguish an apple tree from a fig tree. The rabbi gave this answer: "A new day has arrived when you can look at a human face, and see a brother or a sister. If you are unable to see a brother or a sister in every human face, you are still in the darkness of night."

Though morning had come, for the woman's accusers it is still night. They cannot see that it is their brother and their sister who have committed the sin. They have humiliated the more vulnerable partner of the adultery by making her stand alone in the public temple area. This echoes the malice of the elders who ordered the veil to be removed from the woman Susanna after accusing her of adultery (Dan 13:32).

Moreover, in their darkness, the woman's accusers are unable to see that Jesus is also their brother, sent by God to bring them into the light. They have violated the God-given dignity of the woman by reducing her to the status of an object. They attempt to use her as a means to advance their own interests by laying a trap for Jesus in order to have a charge to bring against him. The malice of their action is compounded by the fact that they are seeking to destroy Jesus under the guise of honoring the divine law given to Moses. This surely is taking the name of God in vain (Ex 20:7).

We can identify with any of the actors of the drama. Regrettably we can easily identify with the woman's accusers. We too take the name of God in vain when, under the guise of defending some orthodox doctrine or practice, we engage in destructive, personal attacks upon those who differ with us. The woman caught in adultery? We can all identify with her, in need of forgiveness—often fallen from the pure joy of living in harmony with God's truth and love. "What is our innocence, what is our guilt? All are naked, none is safe" (Marianne Moore).

Most important of all, because we share the gift of his Spirit, we can be like Jesus in his act of true judgment and creative love. Forgiveness is true judgment and creative love. We say, for example, that a friendship has ended because some infidelity has destroyed it. The friendship can come into being again through forgiveness, creative love given and received. Jesus re-creates the woman into her beauty as divine image through his forgiveness. He tells her the good news that she is free to walk away from the mess she is in and begin a new life: "Go, [and] from now on do not sin any more."

Campion P. Gavaler, O.S.B.

Passion Sunday
Luke 22:14-23:56

Gospel Summary

The gospel for this Sunday is Luke's version of the passion and death of Jesus. It begins with the Last Supper and the institution of the Eucharist and then continues with the betrayal, the trials before Caiphas and Pilate, and ends with the crucifixion. We recognize this account as the climax of the mission of Jesus and yet it is almost too much to comprehend. Moreover, the homily will need to be short in view of the blessing of palms and the length of the gospel; hence the need to look for the essential kernel of this story.

It is clear that the suffering of Jesus is the most prominent feature of the passion story. However, it is necessary to insist that this story is not primarily about suffering: it is about loving. It was Jesus' love for us that brought him to his passion and early death, and it was his love for us that opened the way for our redemption. The suffering was a consequence of his loving. There are many kinds of suffering, but only the suffering that comes from loving and remaining faithful is redemptive.

Jesus insists on this when he "defines" himself at the Last Supper as "body-broken-for-us" and as "blood-poured-out-for-us." And in the verses that follow he separates himself from his bickering disciples with the simple and profound statement, "I am among you as the one who serves" (22:27).

Life Implications

As Christian disciples of Jesus, we all need to pay close attention to his wisdom and to guide our lives accordingly. Since we tend to be repelled by images of suffering, there is a real danger that we will become too selective in seeking that wisdom. In this way, we may miss the whole point of the passion story.

Today's gospel is a clear reminder that the heart and soul of the wisdom of Jesus is found in this story of his passion and death.

Since his suffering came from his unselfish loving, it follows that we must try to discern the causes of our own suffering. Not all suffering comes from loving. Indeed, it is far more likely to come from frustration or disappointment because we cannot have everything we want.

To walk with the suffering Christ is to feel the pain that inevitably accompanies the kind of love that sacrifices for the sake of others. Good parents do this for their children and good children love and obey their parents, even when it means giving up something they want. Good teachers sacrifice for their students also. Loving presence can easily mean a change of personal plans, so that a loving person is often justified in saying, "My life is no longer my own".

The amazing thing about this kind of loving is that, though it is often very painful, there is a joy in it also. This should not surprise us because, after all, we were created to become free through the love of others and then to convert that precious freedom into loving service. Nothing is more compatible with our true nature as God's children than this kind of loving...and nothing is finally more successful than the resurrection victory that follows such generous and faithful concern for others.

Demetrius R. Dumm, O.S.B.

Easter Season

Easter Sunday

John 20: 1–9

Gospel Summary

On that first Easter Sunday, Mary Magdalene goes to the tomb of Jesus early in the morning and sees that the stone had been removed from the tomb. She runs to get Simon Peter and the disciple whom Jesus loved, and tells them what she saw. Simon Peter and the other disciple enter the tomb to find burial cloths there and the cloth that had covered the head of Jesus. The beloved disciple sees and believes. The gospel passage continues, reaching its climax in subsequent verses with the appearance of the Risen Lord to Mary Magdalene after the two other disciples had gone home.

Life Implications

Today is the day of Easter joy. Yet, even as we celebrate we are painfully aware that for many people it is still Good Friday. Every day it seems there is something to remind us of the poverty, injustice, and violence of our world. Reflecting on his own experience of life, Pope John Paul II in an address to pilgrims in Rome used apocalyptic images: "If we cast a glance at the world...it seems that horsemen are riding through the barren lands of the earth, bearing now the crown of victorious power, now the sword of violence, now the scales of poverty and famine, now death's sharp sickle." We are aware that our Easter celebration is an affirmation of hope in a world that appears to experience the pain of Good Friday more than the joy of Easter Sunday.

Jean-Paul Sartre, a much-read atheist philosopher of a few decades ago, in his play *No Exit* gives us one of the most tragic images of what it means to live in a world without hope and without joy. Three characters of his play, having been condemned to hell, are led by a valet into a pleasant drawing room. Surprised by the absence of fire and brimstone, they remark how nice a place hell has turned out to be. Gradually, however, they begin to get on each other's nerves and at each other's throats. They decide not to speak to each other, but they are stuck with each other. There is nowhere else to go. Finally they realize that they themselves are each other's hell. "Real torture is having no escape, real hell is having no hope."

The three characters of the Easter gospel, representing all of us, experience Jesus, not as the "other" who is their hell, but as their friend who knows them and loves them beyond measure. Mary Magdalene remains at the tomb after the two other disciples went home. Jesus appears to her as she weeps, and says to her, "Mary!" She turns to him and says, "Rabbouni" (which means My Teacher). The tender exchange of recognition between Jesus and Mary Magdalene is the Easter revelation of authentic human existence.

We can celebrate Easter in hope and in joy because Jesus, the Risen Lord, is with us. He knows us, and with affection calls each of us by name. Through the Easter gift of sharing his new life and liberating love, we too can recognize and treat each other with justice and with affection. Easter means that we can be heaven for each other, a source of hope and joy in our No Exit world. We can thank God and sing the Easter song together: "Yes, Christ my hope is arisen...our new life obtaining."

Campion P. Gavaler, O.S.B.

Second Sunday of Easter
John 20: 19–31

Gospel Summary

It is surely an understatement to say that the disciples were filled with joy as Jesus appeared to them, alive and well, on that first Easter day. It will take years for them to draw out all the wonderful implications of this dramatic moment in their lives but for now it is sheer joy. Jesus then gives them a mandate to bring peace to the world by translating their happiness into the difficult but rewarding gift of forgiveness.

The story of "doubting Thomas" is presented as a warning to those of us who have trouble trusting the spiritual side of life. Thomas is called the "twin," possibly because he had a striking physical resemblance to Jesus, but he discovers that this does not give him any advantage at all. What counts now is a spiritual relationship. We often assume that those who knew Jesus in the flesh had a great advantage over the rest of us and we may even envy them. In fact, however, the risen Lord is far more present to us now in the Spirit than he ever was in the flesh.

Finally, the author of the gospel reminds us that everything he has written is intended, not primarily to give us information about Jesus, but rather to bring us to faith in him and thereby to lead us to real "life in his name."

Life Implications

The last verses of this gospel passage are among the most challenging passages in the entire gospel. In the first place, we are told that the whole gospel of John is intended to bring us to "believe that Jesus is the Messiah, the Son of God." This does not mean simply that we accept the fact that Jesus is the fulfillment of Israel's hopes and, much more than that, the very Son of God, equal to the Father and the Holy Spirit. To believe in Jesus means also that we accept the message, found in his words and in his example, of total self-giving for the sake of others. When we truly accept this message, we pledge ourselves to live and love as much as possible as Jesus did.

What is the consequence of such a radical way of living? It enables us to participate in the very life of Jesus. As the gospel puts it, the whole purpose of believing is that "you may have life in his name." This statement is far more daring and revolutionary than we may think. For it means that, through love of others, we begin to participate in the love and life of God. To love unselfishly is to love as God loves, and that means sharing in God's life, insofar as mere creatures can do so.

In other words, we are invited to share in a life that is far superior to the fragile, uncertain life of our mortal existence. This new life is given in baptism but it must be nourished by our commitment to loving service and by our participation in the Eucharist, the ultimate sacrament of love and concern for others.

St. Paul expresses the same conviction when he writes those wonderfully consoling words: "Therefore, we are not discouraged; rather although our outer self is wasting away, our inner self is being renewed day by day" (2 Cor 4:16). This inner renewal is nothing less than the growth of God's life within us.

Demetrius R. Dumm, O.S.B.

Third Sunday of Easter
John 21:1-19

Gospel Summary

Simon Peter and his companions after fishing all night catch nothing. At dawn as they approach shore, someone on the shore whom they do not recognize directs them to cast out their net. When the net is filled with a large catch, the beloved disciple recognizes Jesus, now risen from death, and says to Peter, "It is the Lord." When they reach shore, they see a charcoal fire with fish on it and bread. Jesus invites them to eat with him. He takes bread and gives it to them and in like manner the fish. Jesus then asks Peter three times if he loves him, and says to him in turn, "Feed my lambs...Tend my sheep...Feed my sheep." Jesus then speaks of the kind of death Simon Peter will undergo, and says to him, "Follow me."

Life Implications

Friendship with Jesus is the one essential thing of life, regardless of any other circumstance—sickness or health, poverty or wealth, low or high position in society or church. That is the supreme truth John wants to tell us in his gospel. The good news is that Jesus desires our friendship, and offers it to all who welcome him in faith. We can identify with many of the persons Jesus encounters in the gospel—the Samaritan woman, Martha and Mary, Lazarus (at whose death Jesus wept), Peter, Mary Magdalene, the beloved disciple. The gospel also warns us not to identify with those who reject friendship, and even betray friendship with Jesus. Jesus can also call us his friends because he has told us everything he has heard from his Father (Jn 15:15). The titles that we use to address Jesus (Messiah, Lord, Son of God), however orthodox and exalted they may be, are inadequate to express the full meaning of Jesus for us unless they include "Beloved Friend."

A personal, loving relationship with the Risen Lord clearly was a distinguishing characteristic of John's community. Sad experience, however, soon revealed that individual relationships with Jesus were not sufficient to hold the community together. We can see from the First Letter of John that various individuals, claiming to speak with the Spirit of Jesus, began to teach false doctrines. Eventually they formed splinter groups that separated people from the community. In our gospel passage today, John shows us that individual friendships with Jesus must be complemented by authority within the community. The Risen Lord commissions Peter to serve that function.

That authority that Jesus gives, however, must be exercised out of deep friendship with him. "Do you love me?" Jesus asks Peter the crucial question three times as he commissions him to tend and to feed his sheep. The principle, of course, applies not only to the successor of Peter, but to everyone who exercises authority in the church, from the family to the chancery. Only in this way does human authority becomes an expression of the authority of Jesus, the Good Shepherd who lays down his life for his sheep.

In today's gospel passage, John also links friendship with Jesus with his real presence at our Eucharistic meal. The meal Jesus shares with his disciples together with the feeding of the large crowd (John 6) and the Last Supper Discourse reveal the meaning of the Eucharist for us. Jesus, the Risen Lord, truly is with us at our sacred meal— speaks to us, prays with us, leads us in self-giving to the Father, gives himself to us as our bread and wine. He calls us his disciples and his friends: the life implications remain the same. Jesus also says to us: "If I, therefore, the master and teacher, have washed your feet, you ought to wash one another's feet" (John 13:14). The way we will fulfill his request to follow him as disciples in service of others is unique and particular for each of us. We can count on the Spirit of Jesus to guide us in discerning what that service will be.

Campion P. Gavaler, O.S.B.

Fourth Sunday of Easter
John 10:27-30

Gospel Summary

In order to appreciate fully the import of this beautiful gospel passage, we need to pay close attention to the context. Earlier in chapter ten, Jesus had called himself the good shepherd and then defined a good shepherd as one who loves his sheep and is prepared to die for them. Sheep herding, contrary to some popular conceptions, is a hard and lonely life, but the true shepherd loves his work and gladly accepts many sacrifices in order to keep his flock safe and sound.

When Jesus says, therefore, that "My sheep hear my voice; I know them, and they follow me," he is assuming that the sheep already know how completely he has earned their trust. The sheep hear his distinctive call and follow him, not just because he is an authority figure in their lives, but because he has been such a good shepherd to them.

This example is, of course, only a metaphor for us Christians who belong to the spiritual flock of Jesus. We are assumed to have experienced his love and to know him so well that we implicitly trust his message as well as his promise of eternal life.

Life Implications

To belong to the spiritual flock of Jesus is to hear his voice. This means much more than simply reading or hearing about him. Such information is always helpful, but the decisive moment comes when we go beyond external testimony and begin to discover Jesus at the center of our lives in a profoundly intuitive and trusting manner.

In the analogy that Jesus uses, we can be sure that the sheep who hear their shepherd's call do not go through some "rational" process before deciding to respond. On the contrary, there is, ever so gradually, an instinctive and whole-hearted recognition of the call and a total trust in the concern and devotion of the one who has already demonstrated his love and care for them.

In the case of us Christians, this is a spiritual bond that can be stronger than death. As Jesus tells us, nothing and no "one can take them out of my hand." The only precondition on our part is that we continue to trust the "way of Jesus," which means that we use our freedom and strength to be a loving, caring presence in our world. We can do this most effectively in the context of a supportive community and with the nourishment of the Eucharist.

When Jesus concludes by making the dramatic claim that "the Father and I are one," he is not just assuring us of his equal status in the Trinity of divine Persons. Rather, he is confirming that the life that he offers to us is the same life that he shares with the Father. This is made clear when he says, in the context of the Eucharist, "Just as the living Father sent me and I have life because of the Father, so also the one who feeds on me will have life because of me" (6: 57). It is divine and unending life that the good shepherd wants for us and we can be sure of having that life if we pass on to others the same selfless love that he has shown to us.

Demetrius R. Dumm, O.S.B.

Fifth Sunday of Easter
John 13:31-33a, 34-35

Gospel Summary

Jesus tells his disciples in this passage from the Last Supper Discourse that now he is glorified, and God is glorified in him and will soon glorify him further. Jesus says that he will be with them only a little while longer. Then Jesus gives them a new commandment: "As I have loved you, so you also should love one another." This is the sign whereby people will be able to recognize disciples of Jesus—their love for one another.

Life Implications

The word "glory" appears about 375 times in the Old Testament and about 175 times in the New. The key to grasping its elusive meaning is to understand that, like a sacramental sign, its purpose is to create or to deepen personal relationship. "The heavens declare the glory of God ... all the earth is filled with glory" (Ps 19:2 and Is 6:3). It is possible, however, for an individual to express deep awe in the presence of the beauty of the heavens and the earth, yet not recognize the beauty as a gift of God's glory. For its inter-personal meaning to be realized, glory (like a sacrament) must at the same time be objectively given and subjectively received. To recognize the glory of divine presence in gratitude—now doubling the meaning of the term—is to give glory to God.

The Gospel according to John tells the good news that Jesus is the complete, human manifestation of God's presence among us: he is the glory or sacramental sign of the divine presence. John structures his gospel around seven major signs or expressions of divine glory: changing water to wine at the wedding feast ("Jesus did this as the beginning of his signs in Cana in Galilee and so revealed his glory, and his disciples began to believe in him" [Jn 2:11]); cure of the noble's son; cure of the paralytic; feeding the multitude with bread; showing power over the sea; giving sight to the blind man; raising Lazarus from death.

Through these signs some began to recognize the divine presence in him. Others, however, remained blind and did not perceive these events as the presence of God's glory.

In his farewell address, Jesus speaks of the eighth event that will be the summary and climax of the seven previous signs. This will happen when he is lifted up for all to see, giving himself in love even to death on a cross. This sign is the ultimate revelation that God is love—the complete expression of God's glory. God is thus manifested or glorified in him. Jesus on the cross declares the supreme glory of God to be love. God then glorifies him through resurrection.

The Last Supper context of today's passage reminds us that now in every time and place, the Risen Lord extends the eighth sign of divine love through the Eucharist. The bread and wine do not hide, but express the glory of Christ—the sacrament of his giving himself to us out of love just as he gave himself to us on the cross. Only through the seeing of faith can we recognize the glory manifested as Jesus gives himself on the cross and now gives himself to us as bread and wine.

It is no surprise to discover that Jesus asks all who believe in him to do what he has done to manifest God's glory. If we love others as he has loved us, if we become bread and wine for others, what we say and what we do become expressions of divine glory and signs of the divine presence. Through love that we give, people will know that we are disciples of Jesus. And perhaps in our age of disbelief, through the miracle of love, people may begin to believe in the divine presence, though heretofore they had not perceived the heavens and the whole earth to be filled with divine glory.

Campion P. Gavaler, O.S.B.

Sixth Sunday of Easter
John 14:23-29

Gospel Summary

When Jesus says, in today's gospel, "Whoever loves me will keep my word," he wishes to remind us that, though it is easy to say that we love him, it is far more difficult to obey him by offering our love to our fellow humans. Such concern for others will be the indispensable proof of our authentic love of Jesus, for to love Jesus means ultimately to commit oneself to imitate his unconditional love of others.

This challenge is very difficult, and may even seem impossible at times, but our feeble efforts will be strengthened by the love of the Father—the same divine Father whose love is revealed in Jesus. And when we allow that divine love to flow through us, we will discover that both Jesus and the Father will make their dwelling with us in an ineffable mystical communion. Nothing could be more desirable.

Jesus promises to send us the Advocate, which is the special name John gives to the Holy Spirit. An advocate is one who stands with another to take away that person's fear and sense of aloneness or inadequacy. This divine Advocate will thus dwell deep within us and will continue the work of Jesus by drawing out all the implications of his teaching.

Life Implications

John's gospel is full of reminders that Jesus has come among us to reveal the true nature of God as one who cherishes his love far more than his power. It is for that reason that Jesus is called the Word of God, for he reveals what is hidden in God just as our words make known our hidden thoughts.

When we accept in faith the testimony of Jesus about the love of God for us, we are liberated from the need to worry excessively about ourselves and are thus enabled to become more and more aware of others and more ready to share our love with them. When this happens, we are drawn into that powerful flow of life and love which courses between the Father and Jesus. In this sense, we can understand how the Father and Jesus will "make their dwelling" with us. When this happens, we discover for the first time the real meaning of our lives, for we will then become what our creator has always intended us to be.

The Advocate/Spirit is given to us, therefore, as one who stands at our side, in bright days and dark, to help us understand the reality of this love of God that Jesus offers to us. As we do so, we will become ever more united with Jesus who has revealed the Father's love and who wishes to lead us back to the source of that love. It will be only then that we will begin to understand the meaning of coming home.

Demetrius R. Dumm, O.S.B.

Ascension of the Lord
Luke 24:46-53

Gospel Summary

The feast of the Ascension celebrates the departure of the Risen Lord from this world to the place reserved for him in heaven. As such, it is the continuation of his Resurrection and the completion of his victory over the forces of sin and death.

In Luke's gospel account, the Ascension takes on special meaning because it not only signals the end of the earthly sojourn of Jesus but also prepares for the continuation of his work of salvation in the Acts of the Apostles, which is Luke's sequel to his gospel. We recall that Luke's gospel is dominated by the "journey" of Jesus from Galilee to Jerusalem (9:51-21:38). Jerusalem is like a magnet for his ministry because it is there that we find the temple, representing God's presence, and the altar, prepared for the ultimate sacrifice of Jesus.

This sacrifice of Jesus in Jerusalem seems to be the end of his career but in fact it releases the power of the Spirit, which flows from Jerusalem to the farthest corners of the earth. Though Jesus does indeed "leave" his disciples when he ascends to heaven, he assures them that he is sending the "promise" of his Father upon them. This is the Holy Spirit who will guide and strengthen them (and all of us) for witnessing to Jesus, in word and deed, everywhere in the world.

Life Implications

Those of us who follow Jesus belong to the period of the Church. Through preaching and the sacraments, the Church strives to make Jesus present among us so that we may be empowered to bear witness to the power of God to deliver us from the bondage of sin and despair. It is the Holy Spirit who guides and supports us as we attempt to live the ideals of our calling and to introduce others to the salvation won for us by the sacrifice of Jesus.

One of the principal roles of this Holy Spirit is to enable us to recognize how to live as Jesus did in circumstances that are far removed from the situation in first century Israel. It is the role of the Spirit to tell us then what Jesus would do if he were living here in the twenty-first century. Such guidance will not only give us courage and confidence but it will also enable us to understand what unselfish love means in difficult and worrisome situations.

It is truly remarkable that the disciples in the gospel story do not grieve when Jesus leaves them. Instead, they "returned to Jerusalem with great joy, and they were continually in the temple praising God" (Luke 24:52-3). As we live in the Spirit and try to be sensitive to the Spirit's promptings, we too can be filled with joy and find it fitting to express that joy with words of praise and thanksgiving. As we do so, we will surely attract others who will want to know our secret and will thus be ready to learn about the wonderful gift of salvation won for us by the love of Jesus.

Demetrius R. Dumm, O.S.B.

Seventh Sunday of Easter
John 17:20-26

Gospel Summary

This Sunday's gospel passage contains part of the prayer Jesus addressed to his Father following his Last Supper discourse with its the promise of the holy Spirit. Jesus prays for his disciples and for all who will believe in him through their words. The depth and poetic beauty of Jesus' prayer defies making an adequate prose summary. Principal elements of the prayer are listed here merely as an aid to memory for the reader—communion in the life of Father and Son, desire that the world come to believe in him, desire that all may see his eternal glory, desire that the Father's love be in all who believe.

Life Implications

We usually associate the presence of the Spirit that Jesus gave to his disciples after the resurrection with the audacity with which they preached the gospel (the parrhesia of Acts 4:13,29,31). The first reading of today's liturgy from the Acts of the Apostles alludes to that understanding in recounting the story of Stephen ("filled with the holy Spirit") who was enabled to follow Jesus with courage even to death in his martyrdom. Our gospel passage perhaps is even a more striking illustration of the belief that Jesus shares his Spirit with the church.

What could be more audacious than to express in words the intimate communion of Jesus with his Father in prayer as today's gospel passage does? The church today continues to pray with the Spirit of Jesus, particularly in its eucharistic liturgy. The Spirit also guides each of us in our unique, individual prayer so that we may become more aware that Jesus lives and prays in us. And the Spirit enables us to live in the awareness that the Father loves us with the same love that he loves Jesus. (Raymond E. Brown in his commentary on the fourth gospel calls this last implication of Jesus' prayer "breathtaking.")

The prayer of Jesus is not past tense: as Risen Lord Jesus prays in the eternal now with the same desire of love, and invites us to pray with him in company with all the angels and saints. This is the truth that the second reading of today's liturgy from the Book of Revelation calls to our attention. And this is the truth Saint Augustine taught newly baptized Christians in his Easter Sunday sermon of the year 415. In the Eucharistic liturgy we already now are participants with the Risen Lord in the liturgy of heaven. "You are urged to lift up your hearts. That is only right for the members of Christ. If the head had not gone ahead before, the members would never follow. So our head is in heaven. That is why, after the words 'Lift up your hearts,' you reply, 'We have lifted them up to the Lord'."

Jesus continues to pray that all may be one just as the Father and he are one in order that the world may come to believe. In Jesus' mind, the unity and love among his followers will draw all people to believe in him. The separation and hostility among Christians surely is a scandal in the strictest sense—an obstacle to belief. "See how they attack one another" seems so often to have replaced the saying of pagans about Christians in the ancient world, "See how they love one another." We might recall that at the Last Supper Jesus was aware that he would soon become the innocent victim of violence. Nevertheless, Jesus refused to save himself by responding to violence with "sacred" violence, however justified that response might appear. He experienced God as loving; therefore, he could not be anything else. He knew that even "sacred" violence results only in deeper separation and deeper hostility. It cannot transform the human heart. Only the Father's love in Jesus and in us can work that supreme miracle.

Campion P. Gavaler, O.S.B.

Pentecost Sunday
John 20: 19–23

Gospel Summary

There seems to be a contradiction between the coming of the Spirit as recorded in this gospel and in the first reading from the Acts of the Apostles. In the gospel, the Spirit is given by Jesus himself on Easter day, whereas in Acts the Spirit comes upon the disciples at the Jewish feast of Pentecost which occurred fifty days after Passover (2:1-4). This dilemma appears to be resolved when we recall that the Spirit was also given to the prophets of the Old Testament. After the resurrection of Jesus, it is the fullness of the Spirit that is offered to us, and this can happen in various ways and on many occasions.

What matters most is to understand the implications of this out-pouring of God's Spirit. This is clearly presented in today's gospel where the new presence of Jesus in the Spirit is expressed in terms of peace, mission and forgiveness. The risen Lord addressed his disciples with the greeting, "Peace." However, this is no longer just a wish, as is the case when we use it as a greeting; it is now a GIFT. Living in the Spirit of Jesus will provide us with a deep confidence that can withstand even the most tragic experiences.

To live in the Spirit of Jesus means also to accept the mission of making the love of the Father evident in our world and thereby to continue and to extend the presence of Jesus in human history. The love of Jesus is made present in our world most effectively through the loving presence of his followers.

Jesus then breathes upon the disciples, just as God had done in the creation story (Genesis 2:7), making clear that the new life in the Spirit will be a challenge to us just as it was to Adam--a challenge that will lead to life or death. Some will accept the message of Jesus with joy and be converted and experience forgiveness. Others will resist the good news as they cling to selfish ways and thus remain in sinful rebellion.

Life Implication

Many years ago, I heard one of our older monks say about a young novice, "That one has the Spirit." What he seemed to suggest was that this novice was imbued with such a spirit of quiet, confident joy that he was able to go about his work and prayer in a way that seemed so natural and so spontaneous that it could almost be called instinctive. He was reveling in life, not enduring it.

That novice had, of course, the great advantage of being young and healthy. But we all know older persons also who have experienced the sorrows as well as the joys of life and who still seem so peaceful and confident. This cannot be simply a matter of personal disposition. This can only happen when we open ourselves fully to the Spirit of God.

When we live in this positive and loving way, we are fulfilling the mission of Jesus in our world. We may seem to be warming and redeeming only the small, chilly space that we happen to occupy in life but our kindness radiates in fact in wonderful ways to touch the whole world. This loving concern will also include the precious gift of forgiveness—a gift that heals and reconciles and liberates. To be a follower of Jesus is a blessing; to "have the Spirit" is the fullness of that blessing.

Demetrius R. Dumm, O.S.B.

Ordinary Time

Baptism of the Lord
Luke 3:15-16, 21-22

Gospel Summary

The first verses of today's gospel make it clear that the baptism of John is only a preparation for the coming of Jesus. His baptism is in water only, whereas the baptism that Jesus offers is also "with the Holy Spirit and fire" (Luke 3:16). This is a reference no doubt to the transforming power of the Holy Spirit at Pentecost which is fully described in Luke's other book, the Acts of the Apostles (see chapter 2).

Luke's description of the baptism of Jesus is very similar to that of Matthew and Mark. First of all, the heavens are opened, signaling the end of that centuries-long apparent absence of God. Now that Jesus is on the scene, it is time to initiate that final act in the drama of God's coming to save his people. The appearance of the dove represents symbolically the advent of a new creation, just as the dove signaled for Noah the end of the flood and a new era of God's grace (Gen 8:8-11).

The climax of this scene comes with the voice from heaven, which tells us in effect that the new creation will involve an influx of divine love that will be incarnate in the person of Jesus. Henceforth, he will be the embodiment among us of God's transforming and empowering love with a potential to transform the universe.

Life Implications

This description of the consequences of the baptism of Jesus must not be seen simply as something that happened to Jesus alone. For in our own baptism we have become part of the new creation and God speaks to us also with those same loving and empowering words that he spoke to Jesus (adapted to our situation): "You are my beloved child; I love you very much." With these divine words we are truly joined to the person and the mission of Jesus.

The fact that we cannot hear these words in a conscious way when we are baptized as infants makes it all the more important that we learn how to listen as we grow older and become more aware of the presence of God. In fact, there is nothing that we can do during our lives that is more important than listening as God tells us, in our hearts and souls, that we are his beloved and cherished children. We are bombarded constantly by the words of our busy world and some of them may be important, but none of these human words can possibly be as important in our lives as the words of God spoken to us in our baptism.

There can be no doubt that Jesus heard these words of his heavenly Father all during his ministry. When he went aside to pray, he would be comforted and reassured and strengthened by these loving words. We too would do well to set aside some time each day to listen as God whispers to us that we are so loved that we do not ever need to be afraid. As we do that, we enter into the full meaning and power of our baptism and we find the secret of living in gratitude and hope, as we prepare for resurrection glory.

Demetrius R. Dumm, O.S.B.

Second Sunday in Ordinary Time
John 2: 1-11

Gospel Summary

There are several unusual features about this story in today's gospel. First of all, it is not customary for Jesus to perform a miracle merely to help friends avoid embarrassment. Secondly, this is the only time in John's gospel that we see the mother of Jesus intervene to ask a favor of her Son. Finally, Jesus addresses his mother as "woman," which is not the way one addresses one's mother, then or now.

All of these features warn us to be alert for symbolic meaning in this story. This should not surprise us, for symbolism has always been the language of religion. It gives wings, as it were, to earth-bound words so that they can rise to the level of divine meaning. Thus, contrary to what many suppose, symbolic interpretation is not opposed to what is "real" or "historical;" it is opposed to what is spiritually meaningless!

And so, when Jesus calls his mother "woman," he is recognizing in her the role of new Eve, "mother of all the living" (Gen 3:20), because she is his mother and he represents a new creation. When Jesus resists her request because his "hour has not yet come," we are reminded of the only other place in John's gospel where Jesus addresses his mother as "woman," and that is when his "hour" has in fact arrived (19:26-27). At that time, Mary, suffering now with her son on Calvary, becomes mother of all who are inspired by the new life of faith and who accept the wisdom of Jesus about unselfish living.

Life Implications

We can accept as historical fact that Mary gave birth to Jesus. However, she bore him again on the spiritual level when she stood by his cross and became the spiritual mother of the whole Church, whose members are united with him in faith and in the Eucharist, sacrament of love. Thus, although Jesus is willing to respond to the family crisis at that wedding feast, John needs also to remind us that Jesus did not really come to make wine out of water but to save us by the kind of love that includes suffering and death. And his mother will be forever our model as she stands by her Son's cross and embraces his wisdom.

This new life is symbolized by zestful wine and is therefore so much better than the colorless and "watery" life that we experience before conversion. Faith enables us to begin already to experience this new life as we embrace the wisdom of Jesus and Mary. This will mean embracing the cross also because unselfish love is always a little dying, just as it is also learning to live in a "divine" way.

When the gospel tells us "his disciples began to believe in him," it means that they began to see that Jesus alone could offer them the new life that is symbolized by the "good wine" that is saved till the end of the feast. In fact, Jesus has come in these latter days to save us all from the embarrassment of a meaningless existence as he offers us the secret of a truly festive life of gentle sacrifice and generous trust.

Campion P. Gavaler, O.S.B.

Third Sunday in Ordinary Time
Luke 1:1-4; 4:14-21

Gospel Summary

With this passage Luke introduces his two-volume work—Gospel and Acts of the Apostles. Luke's work continues the narrative of God's liberation of humanity from the mess it had gotten itself into, alienated from its creator and alienated within itself. It is a narrative of the creative, divine action of the Spirit beginning with Israel, continued through Jesus, and now through the Church.

After linking the birth of Jesus to the fulfillment of God's promise of blessing for all nations given to Abraham and to Israel, Luke tells us that Jesus returned to Galilee in the power of the Spirit. He teaches in the synagogues to the acclaim of all. Then Jesus goes to Nazareth, where he had grown up, and as was his custom goes to the synagogue on the Sabbath. He stands to read the scroll from the prophet Isaiah: "The Spirit of the Lord is upon me, because he has anointed me to bring glad tidings to the poor ...." Rolling up the scroll, Jesus hands it back to the attendant and sits down. The eyes of all in the synagogue look intently at him. He says to them: "Today this scripture passage is fulfilled in your hearing."

Life Implications

Writing during the fifth decade of the Church's life, Luke wants us to understand that the same Spirit that was upon Jesus also came upon the Church at Pentecost. Peter said in his Pentecost speech: "Exalted at the right hand of God, he received the promise of the holy Spirit from the Father and poured it forth, as you see and hear" (Acts 2:33). All that Jesus began to do through the power of the Spirit during his earthly life he continues to do now as Risen Lord in the Church. It is through the power of the Spirit of Jesus that the Church brings glad tidings of liberation and new life to all the peoples of the world.

Today's gospel passage begins this liturgical year's cycle of readings taken principally from Luke's gospel. I would suggest a reading of Luke's gospel and the Acts of the Apostles comparing how Jesus acted through the power of the Spirit during his earthly life and how he is acting now through the Spirit in our own lives and in the life of the Church. Gerard Manley Hopkins provides a word of encouragement with his observation: "To hear of him and dwell on the thought of him will do us good."

There is an immediate life-implication of today's passage that is easy to overlook. The Spirit of the Lord comes upon Jesus and comes upon the Church in order to bring glad tidings. The presence of the Spirit means joy. In the 21st century we're OK with entertainment and pleasure, but are suspicious of joy because it might be a pie-in-the-sky illusion. How can we talk about joy, or even allow ourselves to experience joy, when there is so much false hope, so much suffering, so much serious work to be done?

Luke and other writers of the New Testament, certainly as aware of suffering as much as we are, did talk about glad tidings and joy. When the holy Spirit came upon her at the Annunciation, Mary sang "My spirit rejoices in God my savior. For he has looked upon his handmaid's lowliness" (Luke 1:47-48). Repeatedly Luke tells us that Jesus was filled with the Spirit. He reports this reaction when Jesus recognized that though many people were rejecting him, Satan would finally be defeated: "At that very moment he rejoiced in the holy Spirit and said, 'I give you praise, Father, Lord of heaven and earth, for although you have hidden these things from the wise and the learned you have revealed them to the childlike'" (Luke 10:21). At the Last Supper when his own suffering was at hand, Jesus spoke of returning to his Father and sending their Spirit: "I have told you this so that my joy may be in you and your joy may be complete" (John 15:11).

The supreme paradox of Christian faith is the cross of Jesus. The cross symbolizes the pain and sorrow that Jesus and we know so well. At the same time, the cross of Jesus is the symbol of joy because it is the ultimate revelation of the love of his sacred heart for us. "For the sake of the joy that lay before him he endured the cross despising its shame, and has taken his seat at the right of the throne of God" (Hebrews 12: 2). The joy that lay before him was not only that God would wipe away his every tear, but that through his self-giving love, his joy might be in us and our joy might be complete.

At our Eucharist today we pray for the gift of anointing in fullest measure by the Spirit so that even in this valley of tears we might share the joy of Jesus' heart. We pray too that as individual Christians and as Church, through the power of the Spirit, we will have the courage to bring glad tidings of great joy to the poor, liberty to captives, sight to the blind, and freedom to the oppressed.

Demetrius R. Dumm, O.S.B.

Fourth Sunday in Ordinary Time
Luke 4:21-30

Gospel Summary

Biblical passages used in the liturgy often suffer from being removed from their contexts. This is particularly noticeable in today's gospel selection, which shows Jesus referring to a biblical passage from Isaiah, which he has just read without telling us what it is. We need to note, therefore, that he has just read an important messianic passage. Accordingly, when he declares that this prophecy has been fulfilled, he is in effect announcing his own claim to be God's chosen one for the liberation of Israel.

Jesus senses some resistance to this dramatic announcement and counters it by reminding them that it is always difficult for local folks to believe that one of their own might be much more than they have given him permission to be. In a sense, this is a recognition of the truth in that adage: "Familiarity breeds contempt."

This narrowness of vision takes on much more serious implications when it touches our own relationship with God. As Jesus points out, God has never felt obliged to recognize privilege based solely on birth (or church membership). Being a member of a chosen people simply clarifies one's obligation to respond to God's special claims on that people; It does not excuse one from obedience to those claims. It is a privilege with heavy responsibilities. Thus, in the gospel story, the widows and lepers from outside of Israel prove to be more worthy of God's attention than the members of his own people.

Life Implications

It is important to recognize the symbolic and universal implications of the narrow-minded attitude of excessively provincial people. The challenge of today's gospel takes us far beyond the merely social implications of that phenomenon. The fact is that we are all tempted to reject the challenging initiatives of God in order to cling to our own more familiar and controllable vision of life. The words of Isaiah are pertinent here: “For my thoughts are not your thoughts, nor are your ways my ways—oracle of the Lord. For as the heavens are higher than the earth, so are my ways higher than your ways, my thoughts higher than your thoughts” (Isaiah 55: 8-10).

This point is sharpened in the words of Jesus to Peter when he reacts against the thought of a suffering and dying Messiah: “You are thinking not as God does, but as human beings do” (Mark 8:33). Jesus is God’s Messiah long before he is our Messiah. And, although we will always be tempted to “domesticate” and make reasonable the claims of God, they will forever challenge us to be converted from self-satisfied, provincial and merely human ways of relating to God’s message.

As a matter of fact, the divine message, embodied in the person and words of Jesus, calls us into the “wilderness” of endless concern for others. For we never really know where unselfish love will lead us. We may even have to say at times, “My life is really no longer my own. I have loaned it to others who are more in need than I am.” When that happens, we will understand why Jesus said that God went outside of Israel to take care of the widow of Sidon and Naaman, the Syrian.

Demetrius R. Dumm, O.S.B.

Fifth Sunday in Ordinary Time
Luke 5:1-11

Gospel Summary

While Jesus was speaking to a crowd that was pressing in on him by the Lake of Gennesaret, he noticed some fishermen washing their nets. He got into one of their boats, the one belonging to Simon, and asked him to put out a short distance from the shore. He then taught the crowd of people from the boat. After he had finished speaking, he told Simon to go out into deep water and lower his nets for a catch. Simon replied that they had worked all night and caught nothing, but he would do as Jesus asked. Simon and his partners caught so many fish that their nets were about to break, and their two boats were completely filled.

When Simon Peter saw this he fell at the knees of Jesus and said, "Depart from me, Lord, for I am a sinful man." Jesus said to Simon, "Do not be afraid; from now on you will be catching men." When they reached shore, Simon and his partners, James and John, left everything and followed Jesus.

Life Implications

One of the most pervasive threats to the faith of Christians during the first centuries of the Church was a religious philosophy called Gnosticism (from a Greek word meaning "to know"). This philosophy rejected the creator God of Genesis for a supreme, unknowable Divine Spirit beyond the God of Scripture. Further, Gnostics taught that all matter, including the human body, was evil. They believed, however, that certain human beings were a spark of the Divine Spirit, and through a secret knowledge could be freed from the prison of their bodily humanness to realize their true, eternal spiritual nature.

In their view, Jesus was a Gnostic, a spark of the Divine Spirit, who only appeared to share the nature and lot of human beings. He, therefore, really did not suffer and die, but came only to teach the secret knowledge to other "spirituals" in the fallen world. In its negation of the material world, Gnosticism was a threat to Christian faith because it seemed to be spiritually superior. The New Testament, on the other hand, stresses the reality of the suffering and death of Jesus in whom "dwells the whole fullness of the deity bodily"(Colossians 2: 9). Jesus endured the shame of the cross, Paul said, and to proclaim Christ crucified was a "stumbling block to Jews and foolishness to Gentiles" (1 Corinthians 1: 23).

The mind-set of Gnosticism remains a pervasive force in American culture. Harold Bloom, Yale professor and perceptive cultural critic, in his book, *The American Religion: The Emergence of the Post-Christian Nation,* maintains that the American religion is Gnostic. With supposedly superior knowledge, the ideal American Hero ultimately feels no need to be guided by the dogmas and moral inperatives of the past or of organized religion. Like the first humans in the Genesis story of the Fall, the heroic individual desire is to be like the gods, determining for oneself what is good and what is evil. Thus, with unlimited rights and freedom, the essential moral imperative is to create one's own meaning and destiny.

In the mind of Jesus, there is no bypassing humanness, either his own humanity or the humanity of the Church. Today's gospel reveals an important moment in the coming-to-be of the Church, a very human, structured society that Jesus intended even during his earthly ministry. Through this society, aptly called his own Body, he would continue his mission in history, not merely for elite spirituals, but for the whole crowd of people pressing in on him. The Church, which Jesus initiated at the beginning of his earthly ministry, he continues to complete as Risen Lord by sending the promise of his Father (Lk 24:49). It will thus be from the abiding presence of Jesus through his Spirit that Peter will again hear the words of today's gospel as he speaks to the crowds at Pentecost: "Do not be afraid; from now on you will be catching men."

For many people today, the humanness of the Church, if not a scandal and foolishness, is often regarded as an obstacle to direct communion with the Divine Spirit. I am sure that many times the successors of Peter have echoed his words in their hearts: "Depart from me, Lord, for I am a sinful man." Yet, the good news is that Jesus has not departed, and has promised never to depart from the Church. And it is through the humanness of the Church, as through the humanness of Jesus, that God finds us and welcomes us to our true home.

Campion P. Gavaler, O.S.B.

Sixth Sunday in Ordinary Time
Luke 6:17, 20-26

Gospel Summary

It is instructive to compare Luke's Beatitudes with those of Matthew (5:2-11). Luke offers just four Beatitudes while Matthew gives us eight. But the four that Luke shares with Matthew are considered the oldest version and contain the essential teaching. Luke also adds four Woes, not found in Matthew, and intended to re-enforce, by contrast, the message of the previous Beatitudes.

The most important word in all the Beatitudes is the subject of the first one, namely, the "poor." This English word, suggesting economic destitution, does not at all capture the full meaning of the Hebrew word from which it is ultimately derived. In that fuller sense, the poor are the "afflicted ones" or, more specifically, the "powerless ones." This often includes the economically destitute but it includes also those who recognize their radical poverty when it comes to the matter of final salvation. In the gospel, the poor stand in contrast to the Scribes and Pharisees who, though themselves far from materially rich, were so "full of themselves" and so smug about salvation that they effectively closed themselves to the free gift of the Kingdom.

In essence, therefore, God gives salvation to those humble ones who know how powerless they really are in spiritual matters and who are ready to turn humbly to God who is more than willing to give them the Kingdom. The "hungry" and the "weeping" and the "persecuted" are variations on the poor ones. The hungry know that only God can satisfy their needs and do not try to place that burden on any merely human creature. The weeping know that God's command to love often leads to grieving...and who love nonetheless. The persecuted, or ridiculed ones, gladly embrace the "foolish" wisdom of unselfish service because they realize that God's gift is only for the generous ones.

Life Implications

The seemingly benign appearance of these well-known Beatitudes conceals a very harsh judgment on many of the attitudes of the secular culture in which we live and by which we are probably influenced far more than we realize. This secular culture (and our natural instincts) lead us to place a very high premium on control. A metaphor for this in our contemporary world is the remote control for our TVs. There is a pleasing sense of power in being able to "zap" advertisements and people on the screen with whom we disagree.

This tendency could be relatively harmless except when we allow it to influence our relationship with God and our attitude toward other people. An excessive yearning for control is clearly a prideful attitude and it is pride, more than anything else, that blocks our access to the free gift of salvation. It can also destroy the delicate fabric of our loving relationship with other people.

The opposite of our passion for control is our willingness to love to the point of vulnerability. Machismo is unhealthy because it is so out of touch with reality. We are living in a dangerous illusion when we think that we must always be in control. The fact is that we do not control the most important realities in life, such as love, happiness and life itself. These are wonderful gifts and we should be happy to accept them as such. When we try to seize them, they inevitably slip through our fingers.

We need to understand the true role of power. It can be very useful but it must always be guided by love. When that happens, we can also let go of it, when the time comes, and thus be ready for the exquisite gift of God's Kingdom.

Demetrius R. Dumm, O.S.B.

Seventh Sunday in Ordinary Time
Luke 6:27-38

Gospel Summary

This passage from the Sermon on the Plain (6:20-49) is the counterpart of the Sermon on the Mount in the gospel according to Matthew (5:1-7:27). The sayings of Jesus which make up the Sermon, in their poetic simplicity and in their challenging complexity, have become part of the world's common language: Love your enemies, do good to those who hate you, bless those who curse you, pray for those who mistreat you...Be merciful, just as your Father is merciful. Stop judging and you will not be judged. Forgive and you will be forgiven. Give, and gifts will be given to you.

Life Implications

The essence of Jesus' mandates is simple enough: Be merciful, just as your Father is merciful...be like God. Everything else follows. If we are like God, there will be love, forgiveness, and generosity—all beyond measure. If one hears these mandates of Jesus in isolation from the entire New Testament, however, one might conclude that they represent an impossible ideal, and thereby may be ignored as impractical. The second reading of today's Mass from Paul's first Letter to the Corinthians provides the necessary context and helps us make sense of Jesus' command to be like God.

In his Letter to the Corinthians, Paul contrasts first man, Adam, with the last Adam, Jesus. First Adam, created in the divine image and likeness, was meant to be like God. Through prideful disobedience, however, Adam rejected his authentic human existence as God's image and likeness. All humankind as a consequence has inherited, and has added to Adam's condition of alienation from God and from all creation. Humanity, stuck in a false value-system, is like an animal trapped in quicksand that has lost its freedom to live as it was meant to live. Part of the tragedy is that humanity has become blind, and believes that its ungodly values reflect what it means to be human.

In contrast to first Adam, Jesus begins a new creation as the New Adam. Created in the divine image and likeness, through his obedience, love, forgiveness and generosity, he is like God—merciful, just as his Father is merciful. The good news is that through the power of God's mercy, which Jesus has come to proclaim, human beings can be liberated from the sorry mess we have gotten ourselves into.

At the beginning of his ministry in the synagogue at Nazareth, Jesus said that the prophecy of Isaiah was fulfilled in him: "The Spirit of the Lord is upon me, because he has anointed me to bring glad tidings to the poor. He has sent me to proclaim liberty to captives and recovery of sight to the blind, to let the oppressed go free, and to proclaim a year acceptable to the lord" (Lk 4:19-19). Those who recognize that they are poor in the deepest sense (in captivity, blind, helplessly oppressed by evil forces of a fallen world) are blessed because they are able to accept the gift of liberation from their enslavement.

Freedom from enslavement, however, is not enough. Liberation from slavery achieves its purpose only if we live according to the freedom of the New Adam, Jesus Christ. "You have been called to freedom; only do not use your freedom as an opportunity for the flesh, but through love be servants of one another." "Stop lying to one another, since you have taken off the old man (Adam) with his practices and have put on the new man, which is being renewed, for knowledge, in the image of its creator" (Gal 5:13 and Col 3:9-10). Because we have been reborn into his image and likeness as New Adam, Jesus can say to us: Be merciful, just as your Father is merciful...be like God.

Campion P. Gavaler, O.S.B.

Eighth Sunday in Ordinary Time
Luke 6: 39-45

Gospel Summary

The parables that Jesus offers in today's gospel have one thing in common. They are all concerned with the qualities required for authentic discipleship. The "blind" who cannot lead others are essentially the same as the hypocrites, who cannot see their own faults but are always ready to point out the shortcomings of others. Those who resist personal conversion are in no position to lead others to conversion. And a false heart cannot be a truthful and effective witness.

What is really at issue here is one's willingness to live in reality. The person who chooses to live in illusion cannot be helpful in leading others to reality, where alone salvation can be found. Jesus chose reality when he took a path of loving service, which led him to pain and death but also to joy and life.

In the real world, our freedom is for loving and caring, but this is often painful. Hence the almost irresistible temptation to create an illusory world where pride and control can dominate and where pain can be avoided, at least temporarily. Jesus urges us to choose instead the reality of a converted heart producing the rich fruit of kindness and gentleness and freedom.

Life Implications

All this can be seen more clearly when we consider some classic illusions and the following list is by no means exhaustive.

There is the illusion of self-sufficiency, which blinds us to the reality of our interdependence. We need others, and they need us. We do not find reality by looking in the mirror or by talking to ourselves or by refusing to hear others.

A common and destructive illusion is that of low self-esteem, which focuses so exclusively on one's shortcomings that one is paralyzed and gradually slips into the tragic situation of victim-hood.

The reality is that we can all contribute something unique and precious, even if it is only a gentle touch or a generous smile.

Then there is the illusion of indispensability, which leads us to believe that we are irreplaceable. Our contribution may be very significant, but it is always a shock to see how quickly we can be replaced, and even more so if our job is simply eliminated.

A particularly dangerous illusion is that of thinking we are not prejudiced. Everyone is prejudiced in some way and the worst prejudice of all is not to recognize the fact of personal bias. These deeply ingrained attitudes can easily distort our vision of life and will cause us to be narrow-minded and judgmental.

Another common illusion is that of immortality, which prevents us from being realistic about health care and which leads to denial or rationalizations in regard to bad health habits. This illusion is especially dangerous among the young, who often take risks that are foolish and life-threatening.

Demetrius R. Dumm, O.S.B.

Ninth Sunday in Ordinary Time C
Luke 7:1-10

Gospel Summary

A Roman military officer who had heard about Jesus sent some Jewish elders to ask him to come and heal his servant who was sick to the point of death. As Jesus was approaching his house, the centurion sent friends with a message to the effect that he was not worthy to have Jesus enter his house. Further, the centurion said that if Jesus gave the order, the servant would be cured. Jesus said in amazement:"I tell you, I have never found so much faith among the Israelites." When the friends returned to the centurion's house, they found the servant to be cured and in perfect health.

Life Implications

When we hear this gospel passage, we may also be filled with amazement to hear Jesus say, "I have never found so much faith among the Israelites." His saying may help us reflect on the meaning of faith, and may even help us broaden our understanding of its meaning. The Gentile centurion is a decent man. He cares for his servant. He loves the Jewish people, and has even built a synagogue for them, apparently without sharing belief in their religious doctrines. He has heard about Jesus, but there is no indication of any profession of faith, like Peter's, that Jesus is the Messiah or the Son of God.

The teaching of Cardinal Newman (1801-1890) that faith means fidelity to truth as one perceives it in the judgment of one's conscience broadens a reduced understanding of faith simply as an affirmation of religious doctrine. To follow the clear imperative of conscience is to obey the will of God—which is the meaning of faith. Jesus praises the faith of the centurion because of his fidelity to truth as perceived by him in his conscience.

The Catechism of the Catholic Church includes a quote from Cardinal Newman teaching that conscience is the voice of God:

"[Conscience] is a messenger of him, who, both in nature and in grace, speaks to us behind a veil, and teaches us and rules us by his representatives. Conscience is the aboriginal Vicar of Christ" (#1778). The Catechism affirms the teaching of Catholic Faith that one must always obey the clear command of conscience—even though a judgment of conscience objectively may be erroneous. Further, the Catechism states that if a human being "were deliberately to act against it, he would condemn himself" (#1790).

Needless to say, Jesus' praise of the Gentile centurion's faith does not negate his own mission or the mission of the church to teach the fullness of truth to all people. After his resurrection, when his own mission on earth was completed and the mission of the church was to begin, Jesus said to his disciples: "All power in heaven and on earth has been given to me. Go, therefore, and make disciples of all nations, baptizing them in the name of the Father, and of the Son, and of the Holy Spirit, teaching them to observe all that I have commanded you. And behold, I am with you always, until the end of the age" (Matthew 28:18-20).

Campion P. Gavaler, O.S.B.

Tenth Sunday in Ordinary Time

Luke 7:11-17

Gospel Summary

As Jesus was about to enter a city called Nain, a man who had died was being carried out through a city gate. He was the only son of his mother, and she was a widow. Jesus, moved with compassion, touched the coffin, and said, "Young man, I tell you arise." When the young man came back to life, Jesus gave him to his mother. All who witnessed the event glorified God, and exclaimed, "A great prophet has arisen in our midst," and "God has visited his people."

Life Implications

This brief gospel story is a literary gem with strong visual images, yet expressing the great universal truths which give unity to the entire biblical tradition of faith. (1) God visits his people from the first moment of their creation. Amazingly, God wants to be with us. (2) More good news is that God understands our fragile human condition, and responds with compassion. (3) God's presence is personal and respectful of human freedom. The human response which God hopes for is a free decision of faith—the hospitality of welcome and gratitude for the divine visit. (4) God's invisible presence becomes visible in our midst in Jesus, not only a great prophet, but the Son of God become flesh and blood, like us in everything except sin.

The compassion of the invisible God is revealed in the human compassion and life-giving action of Jesus. At the same time, we also see in Jesus the revelation of what God intends every human being to become, a particular image of divine, creative compassion. The entire biblical tradition is an expression of this two-fold revelation. The New Testament writings help us gain some insight into the depths of Jesus' humanity by describing the faith of Jesus in various circumstances of his life, particularly in his final trial of faith. "In the days when he was in the flesh, he offered prayers and supplications with loud cries and tears to the one who was able to save him from death, and he was heard because of his reverence" (Hebrews 5:7).

From his childhood, Jesus learned those divinely inspired words of the Old Testament which describe the meaning of friendship with God in faith, hope, and love. "You shall love the Lord, your God, with all your heart, and with all your soul, and with all your strength" (Deuteronomy 6:5). Even in times of distress when God seems to be absent, faith means to hope with unconditional trust that divine love will ultimately prevail. Jesus experienced in his own faith those inspired prayers which he learned as a child and repeated so often in the synagogue. "My God, my God, why have you forsaken me?" (Psalm 22:1) "Into you hands I commend my spirit" (Psalm 31:6). The power of faith is invincible even in the face of a horrible death of Roman crucifixion.

Jesus is as much the principal character in the story of each of our lives as he was in the story of the widowed mother of Nain. In Catholic faith, we celebrate the Eucharist in which Jesus, now Risen Lord, is present and gives himself to us so completely that we share his human-divine life. The life-changing implication of this good news is captured in the words of Saint Paul: "I live, no longer I, but Christ lives in me; insofar as I now live in the flesh, I live by the faith of the Son of God who has loved me and given himself up for me" (Galatians 2:20). For this supreme gift we glorify God, and with gratitude exclaim, "God has visited his people."

Campion P. Gavaler, O.S.B.

Eleventh Sunday of Ordinary Time
Luke 7:36-8:3

Gospel Summary

Luke's gospel is notable for its portrayal of Jesus as one who represents the compassion and forgiveness of God. No doubt this sensitivity of Luke for the generous nature of Jesus came from his own experience as a native of the city of Antioch where he noted the extremes of wealth and poverty and where he noted also that the rich tended to be self-righteous and judgmental and therefore to assume that the poor were sinful just because they were poor.

In this gospel story, Luke draws a sharp contrast between the smug and self-righteous Pharisee who keeps all the rules but does not have the sensitivity to perform the basic acts of kindness toward a guest and the woman who has a reputation for sinfulness but who receives Jesus with loving service. The woman's reputation for sinfulness could be no more than her inability to keep all the prescriptions of the Law due to her poverty. However that may be, there is no doubt that she understands the importance of loving service just as the Pharisee is totally devoid of such sensitivity.

Jesus makes his point by telling a story about two debtors who owed very different amounts but who were both forgiven. The one who was forgiven more was more likely to be more grateful and loving also, We all need to be forgiven at one time or another, and God is more than ready to forgive us also, but the consequences should be loving gratitude and better behavior in the future and especially more readiness to forgive others.

Life Implications

Since it is so difficult to be consistently loving and forgiving persons, we are tempted to take care of the appearances only and thereby to acquire a reputation for virtuous living as we continue to indulge our tendency to be judgmental and unforgiving. I had occasion one time to give a homily on the gospel story about the Pharisee and the publican. To make my point more forcefully, I tried to describe what Pharisees would look like if they were living today in one of our parishes. I noted, for example, that they would certainly attend Mass on Sunday but, on the way home, they would not hesitate to do a critical and negative assessment of other people they had seen at Mass. After the Mass, a man came to the sacristy and said to me: "Father, I think I may be a Pharisee." I was at a loss to respond at first but then I said to him: "My friend, take courage. What you have just said is something that a real Pharisee would never say!"

It is indeed laudable to attend Mass and to take seriously all the rules of good Christian conduct, but all of this careful observance can be spoiled if it is not accompanied by a genuine spirit of love and forgiveness.

Demetrius R. Dumm, O.S.B.

Twelfth Sunday in Ordinary Time
Luke 9: 18–24

Gospel Summary

Jesus asks his disciples what the crowds were saying about him. Then he asked his disciples, "But who do you say I am?' Peter replies, "The Messiah of God." Thereupon, Jesus says, "The Son of Man must suffer greatly...be killed and on the third day be raised." Then Jesus says that anyone who wishes to follow him as a disciple must also be ready to give up his life for his sake.

Life Implications

In this gospel passage, Jesus defines what the mission of the Christ (Messiah) and subsequently of Christian disciples will be. Contrary to popular expectations, Jesus the Messiah will not be the conquering hero who will fix everything that has gone wrong in the world because of human deceit and violence. Certainly Jesus recognizes human suffering, and responds to it with compassion. He provides food for the hungry, he cures the sick, he drives out demons. However, his mission as Messiah is to address the human dilemma on a deeper level. He will address the inauthentic human condition that is the source of the world's injustice and suffering. Jesus will do so as the Son of Man.

To understand what Jesus means by identifying himself as the Son of Man (the Son of Adam or the Human) we have to see it in the context of the entire biblical narrative about the reality of the human condition. In the beginning God creates humans in his image: children of God, not part of God, but like God. Sadly, we do not get a chance to see what authentic human existence looks like. What we do see is inauthentic human existence soon after the beginning. The first humans reject their truth as creatures. Their children continue to kill and to deceive each other until the human is barely recognizable as being and acting like God. "But the earth was corrupt in the view of God and full of lawlessness" (Genesis 6: 11).

Born into a corrupt and lawless world, humans do not have much chance of knowing, much less of living an authentic existence as God's image. Through revelations and covenants with the Hebrew people, we first hear the good news that God does not abandon his estranged children, but will liberate them from their state of inauthentic existence. This dramatic, divine liberation came to be identified with the appearance of an enigmatic figure called Son of Man (Daniel 7: 13-14).

Jesus identifies himself as the Son of Man. Jesus is the Human created in the divine image as the beginning of a New Genesis. In the gospel narratives we now are able to see in Jesus what authentic human existence looks like. Jesus faithfully lives in a relation of covenant love as Son with his Heavenly Father. He overcomes every temptation. He acts in complete union with the Father's love for all of the human family, estranged in exile.

The expectation of the crowds then and now is that Jesus as Messiah would do a quick-fix of the mess that we humans have made for ourselves. This expectation is similar to that of an avaricious, deceitful person who has hurt people and has also gotten himself in debt, and now hopes that the hurt and his debt will be taken care of by some messiah figure. It did not take Jesus long to realize that unless inauthentic human existence is created anew in the divine image, humans will continue to make a mess of things. The avaricious, deceitful person, unless transformed inwardly with a new heart, would soon be repeating his destructive actions. Jesus the Son of Man fulfills his mission as Messiah by authentically living his human existence as Son of God. The Church now proclaims the good news that the Risen Son of Man and Messiah is present among us to create us anew in his own image. In that renewed image of God, we too are enabled to live an authentic human existence as God intended in the creation of the first humans. We learn what that means in the unique circumstances of our lives through the life and teaching of Jesus. By doing so, we will be able to help fix the corruption and lawlessness that fills the earth, rather than adding to it.

Campion P. Gavaler, O.S.B.

Thirteenth Sunday in Ordinary Time
Luke 9:51-62

Gospel Summary

The first verse of today's gospel is a major marker in Luke's story of salvation. Jesus is now ready to be "taken up," i.e. to move toward the final stage of his mission which must happen in Jerusalem. For that reason, "he resolutely determined (lit. set his face) to journey to Jerusalem." For the next ten chapters, Jesus will be on this journey during which he will illustrate the meaning of the journey of faith on the part of his followers of every age. This is clearly a spiritual journey in which theology trumps all merely historical considerations.

This arrangement also reveals Luke's recognition of Jerusalem as a kind of powerful magnetic force draws Jesus to the climax of his mission. For it is in Jerusalem that he will reveal the whole purpose of his life, namely, to die out of love for others. Then, in Luke's second book, the Acts of the Apostles, he will show how the saving power of the Risen Lord radiates out from Jerusalem to transform the whole world.

Life Implications

The first lesson for those who would travel with Jesus is to put aside all initiatives prompted by anger and prejudice. Thus, Jesus rebukes the disciples who want to repay the hostility of the Samaritans with fiery destruction. The second lesson is one of Luke's favorites, namely, that those who would follow Jesus must be willing to let go of all previous attachments. Half-hearted discipleship simply will not be acceptable.

When Luke shows us how Jesus began his career with signs of power in Galilee only to let go of all that as he gave up his life in Jerusalem, he is offering us a dramatic expression of the profound paradox that lies at the heart of Christianity. Jesus freely gives up his power to control as his loving makes him vulnerable and seems to lead only to defeat. But that same loving concern for others releases the power of God within him—a power that easily conquers death and eclipses by far all the earthly power that he had manifested in Galilee.

Our secular culture teaches us to value the power of wealth and politics and intelligence as the ultimate achievement in human life. This kind of power is not to be despised but it must always be subordinated to the only power that is ultimately effective, that is, the power of loving concern. We too may revel in the success of the "Galilean" period of our lives, usually marked by strength and success, but we must come to understand that the only lasting success in life comes from being loved for ourselves and from loving others for their good. This exchange of loving concern has the potential to transform the world, as we see the book of Acts being written over and over again.

This wisdom will also enable us to put aside anger and violence as ways to solve problems. We will be able to accept Jesus' reminder that to "call down fire from heaven" is not the Christian way to deal with difficult people. Moreover, when we really begin to trust the wisdom of Jesus, we will gladly let go of unworthy attachments as we trust more and more the promises of God and begin to run joyfully toward the future. There we will discover that, as the wise adage says: The only gift we can ever keep, is the one we give away!

Demetrius R. Dumm, O.S.B.

Fourteenth Sunday in Ordinary Time
Luke 10:1-12,17-20

Gospel Summary

Earlier in his gospel Luke tells us the intention of Jesus as he begins his ministry: "To the other towns also I must proclaim the good news of the kingdom of God because for this purpose I have been sent"(4: 43). Later when he was accused of driving out demons by the power of Beelzebul he responded, "But if it is by the finger [power] of God that [I] drive out demons, then the kingdom of God has come upon you"(11: 20). Now Jesus appoints seventy-two others whom he sends out with the same mission and purpose as his own. The disciples receive instructions about how they are to carry out their mission: for example, they are to "carry no money bag, no sack, no sandals." There is also an ominous word of warning. Jesus says, "I am sending you like lambs among wolves." He assures them, however, that Satan has fallen. Yet the disciples are to rejoice, not because the evil spirits are subject to them, but because their names are written in heaven—they belong to God.

Life Implications

We try to bring the implications of Luke's gospel to consciousness at a time when many people in the church seem to have lost hope. They are weary, intimidated by the power of secular culture, and often contentious with each other. People feel helpless in face of the pervasive violence and a sub-culture of dehumanizing poverty while the stock market continues to climb. John Paul II called the life-destroying aspect of our modern world the "culture of death." The false value-systems of the world still seem to have control over the way we think and treat each other.

It is also important to remember that the church of Luke's time was much like our own--contention within and persecution without. Peter, Paul and many early followers of Jesus had been executed in the Roman Empire by the time Luke wrote his gospel. Paul's experience, a few decades earlier in Athens, could well have happened in any modern city. After he had proclaimed the resurrection of Christ to the Athenians, the response was mostly ridicule or indifference. Some said, "We should like to hear you on this some other time"(Acts 17: 32). A few men and women, however, came to believe.

If the celebration of the Eucharist today is to renew our beleaguered hope, we like the Twelve and the seventy-two must hear Jesus speaking the words of the gospel personally to each of us. It is we, either as successors of the Twelve or of the seventy-two, who are being sent for the same purpose that Jesus was sent. The seemingly impossible mission to do what Jesus did would paralyze our spirit unless today we also hear Jesus say to us, "Rejoice because your names are written in heaven." We rejoice because we are members of the household and family of God.

What is the reality to which the biblical expression "kingdom of God" points? The expression is richly multifaceted in meaning. The kingdom of God comes into being wherever God reigns, and wherever God's will is done. The kingdom of God is present in persons through whom God acts. It is no surprise that in the early church the kingdom of God soon came to be identified with Christ himself. God reigns in Christ. God's will is done in Christ. God acts through Christ. To proclaim the kingdom of God is the same as to proclaim Christ. In fact, the church from its beginning, by proclaiming the good news of Christ, was being faithful to his mandate to proclaim the kingdom of God.

The kingdom of God has come upon us if God reigns in our hearts, if God's will is done in us, if God acts through us. Sometimes one can sense God's presence in a person or in a community. Thus what the Second Vatican Council says of Christ may also be said of us: "The presence of the kingdom is seen in the words and works, but above all in the person, of Christ himself" (*Lumen Gentium,* #5).

There is a sense of urgency in the words Jesus addresses to us. Even though we are urged to action, it is equally clear that by our own strength we cannot subdue the evil powers of this world and cure its ills. So that we do not forget to trust in God's power in all we do, Jesus tells us to "carry no money bags, no sack, no sandals." We will be able to continue Christ's mission in the particular circumstances of our lives with audacious hope only if we believe that whatever good we do, it is by the finger of God. And when this happens, we can say with Christ, "The kingdom of God is at hand for you."

Campion P. Gavaler, O.S.B.

Fifteenth Sunday in Ordinary Time
Luke 10:25-37

Gospel Summary

The lawyer in today's gospel is not to be confused with the lawyers of our day. He was a student of the Torah--a word which is more properly translated as "instruction" or "revelation." Today, he would be called a theologian. And he asks the question that is primary in the mind of every theologian, namely, how do we human beings achieve the fulfillment intended by our creator? Jesus gives the classic answer from Deuteronomy 6: 5 (love of God) and Leviticus 19: 18 (love of neighbor). Everything else is secondary.

Jesus moves quickly then to illustrate the practical implications of these commands in the story of the Good Samaritan. The contrast drawn is dramatic: the priest and Levite belong to the class of professional men of religion whereas the Samaritan is a member of that generally despised and uneducated group of Jews who were left in Palestine during the Exile and whose religious "purity" was highly suspect.

According to Jesus' story, however, it is this religious outcast who has understood the real meaning of the Torah while the professional practitioners of religion seem concerned only about the external, ritual elements of Judaism. As in the case of the Publican and the Pharisee, Jesus is not suggesting that one should become a Publican or a Samaritan. Rather, he insists that we should be authentic persons who know how to observe the spirit of our religion and not just its externals.

Life Implications

We should note, first of all, that this is only a story. The fact that it never really happened should cause us to focus on its powerful symbolic message. As such, it offers us a sharp lesson about the danger of hypocritical behavior. It is relatively easy to claim an office or a title or hold a membership card, but the only proof of one's religious sincerity and authenticity is the way in which one's religious profession actually changes one's behavior.

In this story, the new behavior is to respond to need regardless of whether we think the one in need deserves our help. Observing religious rituals or even receiving the Eucharist can unfortunately co-exist with self-centeredness and rash judgment. Real conversion demands that our following of Christ include our determination to offer help to others to the best of our ability, which usually means doing all that we think we can...and then a little bit more!

Such Christian behavior does not mean that we should become doormats or must cater to obsessive-dependents. But it does mean that we should be sensitive to the often-hidden needs of others and ready to help in any way we can. Real love will know how to do this wisely and effectively.

We should also note that when obviously Christian persons do not act in accordance with the ideals taught by Jesus, they scandalize others who may well reject Christianity because they are so repelled by those who proclaim themselves Christians. We all recall the challenging words of Jesus: "This is how all will know that you are my disciples, if you have love for one another" (John 13:35).

Demetrius R. Dumm, O.S.B.

Sixteenth Sunday in Ordinary Time
Luke 10:38-42

Gospel Summary

Two sisters named Martha and Mary extend hospitality to Jesus as he stops for a visit while on his journey to Jerusalem. Mary sits beside Jesus as a disciple talking with him. Martha, burdened by much serving, asks Jesus to tell Mary to help her. Jesus instead tells Martha that while she is needlessly worried about many things, there is need of only the one thing that Mary has chosen.

Life Implications

The first reading of this Sunday's Mass is the story of Abraham and Sarah, who offer hospitality to three strangers. Their generosity in meeting the needs of the strangers knows no bounds: rolls made from fine flour, meat from a choice steer, curds and milk. Martha, a true child of Abraham and Sarah, wants to extend the traditional generous hospitality of her people to Jesus by preparing an elaborate meal for him. Jesus tells her that just one thing will be enough--perhaps a dish of yogurt (no need to prepare a tender choice steak). Jesus then uses this simple incident to talk with his two friends about a deeper level of human need and hospitality.

Jesus, also a true son of Abraham and Sarah, certainly would affirm Martha's generosity in meeting his very human need for food. So that we do not miss this point, Luke places the present passage immediately after Jesus' parable about the Good Samaritan, who responds with generosity to the needs of a man who had fallen victim to robbers. To be a disciple of Jesus does mean to respond with generosity to people in need of the basic necessities of life. That's what Jesus himself did, and the Good Samaritan parable remains an essential part of his teaching. The incident of Jesus' visit and his conversation with Martha and Mary became part of the gospel tradition, however, for another reason.

Jesus knew from his own experience about the basic human needs to which Martha with traditional hospitality was responding. However, he was also aware of a deeper human hunger that things like food, drink, shelter, and health cannot satisfy. It is the hunger for personal encounter—the hunger to be in personal communion with another in mutual self-giving. This deepest of all human hungers is satisfied to some degree in human friendship; ultimately, only in friendship with God. Saint Augustine prayed, "You have made us for yourself, O Lord, and our hearts are restless until they rest in you." Julian of Norwich, like so many saints, expressed the same truth, "For by nature our will wants God, and the good will of God wants us. We shall never cease wanting and longing until we possess him in fullness and joy. Then we shall have no further wants." Is it any wonder that Jesus said that Mary had chosen the better part?

How are we to understand the complementarity of Martha's generous hospitality in meeting Jesus' need for food and Mary's longing for personal communion with him? In response, we might follow the way of Jesus. He fed the hungry, cured the sick and expelled demons of every kind as an expression of love. In other words, our love must also become incarnate in whatever we do to meet the needs of others. Thus, our good work—whether cooking a meal or voting for a bill in congress—becomes a sacrament or an effective sign of our self-giving love. Etty Hillesum, a young Jewish woman who died at Auschwitz, expressed a similar understanding when she wrote that in prayer "'God can enter you, and something of 'Love' too...the love you can apply to small, everyday things." Today in our Eucharist we might join in her prayer: "Let me perform a thousand daily tasks with love, but let every one spring from a greater central core of devotion and love" (*An Interrupted Life*).

Campion P. Gavaler, O.S.B.

Seventeenth Sunday in Ordinary Time
Luke 11:1-13

Gospel Summary

Luke's version of the Lord's Prayer is shorter than the more familiar version found in Matthew's gospel. However, all the essential elements are there. We are asked to address God as "Father" because that word, in normal circumstances, suggests to a child both strength and love. This leads us to the rather astounding conclusion that God's supreme power is made available to us through his love.

We are then told to pray for the coming of God's kingdom—the fulfillment of God's loving plan for us—which comes only at the end of time. In the meantime, we will need daily spiritual nourishment so that we may be strong enough and free enough to forgive others as we await in trust the final challenge of faith at the moment of death.

Jesus then makes all this even more explicit by offering us examples of the power of prayer, especially when it is fervent and persistent. We should note, however, that what God promises in response to our earnest prayers is not necessarily that answer that we seek, but rather the "Holy Spirit." This reminds us that the best answer to all prayers is the powerful gift of the Spirit who enables us to love and trust in the most difficult situations of life.

Life Implications

We do not usually find it too difficult to acknowledge the power of God. Creation is proof enough of that. Jesus now asks us to address this all-powerful God as One whose irresistible power is completely in service of his love. This is difficult for us because we experience power so often as domination and violence. Nonetheless, we must continue to call God our loving Father with the sure conviction that eventually our experience will match our words. For we cannot remain hopeful unless we hear, with Jesus, that God's love offers us all of his immense power for our salvation and happiness.

Praying for the coming of God's kingdom does not mean asking God to come and "shape up" all those other folks who are not as upright as we are. Rather, it means that we trust God so much that we want his dream for us to be fulfilled--something that will come about only at the end of time. It is therefore the victory of God's love for which we pray...and that may very well mean forgiveness of our own self-righteousness.

We are asked to pray also for our daily bread. We are on a journey and, like all travelers, we need sustenance. Mostly we need the nourishment of courage and hope, lest we succumb to cynicism and despair. Then we ask our heavenly Father to lift from our shoulders the burden of sinfulness and guilt so that we may make this spiritual journey with wings on our feet. This petition is followed by a solemn pledge to turn our sense of confidence and joy into forgiveness for all our fellow travelers. For only those who are willing to forgive can expect to be forgiven.

The Lord's Prayer is so central to our Christian experience that St. Teresa of Avila is supposed to have said, when asked how to be a true contemplative, You must simply say the Lord's Prayer...but you must say it very, very slowly! The implication is that we will never exhaust the wisdom found in this wonderful prayer which is so special because it was given to us by Jesus himself.

Demetrius R. Dumm, O.S.B.

Eighteenth Sunday in Ordinary Time
Luke 12:13-21

Gospel Summary

While Jesus is teaching a crowd of people, someone asks him to settle a dispute about an inheritance. Jesus refuses to act as a judge in the dispute, and uses the occasion to warn the crowd against all forms of greed or covetousness. He then illustrates what he means by telling a story about a rich man whose land produced a bountiful harvest. The man decided to build large barns to store his grain and other goods. And he thought about the future day when he would say to himself, "Now as for you, you have so many good things stored up for many years, rest, eat, drink, and be merry!" But God said to him, "You fool, this night your life will be demanded of you." The story is a warning for all who store up treasure for themselves, but are not rich in what matters to God.

Life Implications

Jesus' teaching about the deadly sin of covetousness is at the heart of the biblical tradition. David Noel Freedman, in his recent book *The Nine Commandments*, contends that the first nine books of the bible after Genesis tell how Israel from the Exodus to the Exile violated all Ten Commandments and as a consequence suffered God's just punishment: Exodus (idolatry), Leviticus (taking God's name in vain), Numbers (keeping the Sabbath), Deuteronomy (honoring parents), Joshua (stealing), Judges (murder), 1 and 2 Samuel (adultery), 1 and 2 Kings (false witness). Covetousness (the tenth commandment) is the motivating force behind the violation of all the commandments. (This summary is from a review by Daniel J. Harrington, S.J., *America*, March 12, 2001.)

Today's homily could use examples from any of these books to deepen the understanding of Jesus' warning against covetousness. Genesis, particularly the first eleven chapters, also shows how deadly a sin covetousness is. Here the truths that Israel had learned the hard way through the events of its history are revealed to be true for all humanity. Just as covetousness was the motivating force of Israel's violation of the Ten Commandments, so it was also the motivation of Adam and Eve's violation of the commandment God had given to them. The covetousness was expressed in their desire to be like gods. In the account we can also see the connection between covetousness and fear. Sensing their fear of death, Satan had said to Eve, "You certainly will not die." Their fear it seems impelled them to the covetousness that was their downfall.

Covetousness also seems to have made Adam and Eve forget about God as they were about to eat the fruit. They also forgot that they already were like God—created in the divine image and likeness to live and be creative in their beautiful garden of Eden. There is no suggestion of a rebellious, satanic "I will not serve" in the Genesis story of the Fall. Afterwards, God's response seems to be more disappointment than anger, much like the father of the prodigal son who was so covetous of an illusory good life. It is easy to relate to these universal human experiences in our culture of mass production and advertising. We readily succumb to the fear of being "nobodies" and are stimulated to covet all sorts of things that the "somebodies" have, foolishly forgetting what God might think about the matter. Covetousness seems to engender covetousness in others. It is thus not only the original sin, but it is also an *originating* sin.

Covetousness is a deadly sin because it causes us to forget about God, at times to the point of idolatry (Col 3:5). It also causes us to forget about other people except in resentment or envy. Notice that in Jesus' parable, the rich man thinks only of himself—taking it easy, eating, drinking and having a good time. He does not say to himself, "Now that I have all this money, I will feed the hungry, help the widows and orphans, and give my farm-workers a raise." If he had desired to do such things for others, he would have been rich in what matters to God. "The love of money is the root of all evils" (1 Tim 6:10). Money, on the other hand, at the service of love is the root of countless good things. It takes money to feed the hungry, shelter the homeless, heal the sick, do scientific research, or start a business. That love is a good kind of coveting.

At our Eucharist today we might pray that our lives will not be foolish, but will always be in harmony with God's wisdom. In that wisdom, we can work and live without anxiety even though we realize that this night our life may be demanded of us.

Campion P. Gavaler, O.S.B.

Nineteenth Sunday in Ordinary Time
Luke 12:32-48

Gospel Summary

The very first verse of today's gospel reading tells us exactly why the gospel is Good News. Jesus calls us his "little flock" because he knows how powerless we sometimes feel in a world where violence is so prevalent. But we are also told not to fear, because our heavenly Father is pleased to give us the kingdom. It is precisely because we rely on love and generosity rather than on control and violence that we are eligible for this most precious gift of the "kingdom," that is, ultimate freedom and happiness.

To rely on the way of love and kindness, which often appears so unpromising, is in fact to lay up an "inexhaustible treasure in heaven." The danger is that this way of living can often look like so much "pie in the sky." And that is why the remainder of this gospel reading focuses on the need for vigilance. The moment we are distracted from the wisdom of Jesus, we begin to slip back into the ways of the world, that is, we begin to forget what human life is all about.

To be vigilant means, therefore, to keep Jesus and his teaching constantly before our eyes. We recall that, in the garden of Gethsemane, when Jesus returned to his disciples and found them sleeping, he warned them to "watch and pray" (Mark 14:38). He could just as easily have said, "Watch, that is, pray." For it is only our prayerful remembrance of God's presence among us and of the promise of the kingdom that will protect us from the fateful distractions that lead us to live by the world's standards and to be found unprepared when the Lord comes for us.

Life Implications

We live in a world where the pace of life is far quicker than it was at the time of Jesus. Our planes and automobiles are designed to go faster and faster. Even our medications must work ever more quickly. Sometimes we seem to be in a whirlwind and it is almost impossible to keep our bearings. All of this makes it much more difficult to live in the kind of peaceful world where the voice of God can be heard. Nor is it possible to find such a serene existence without a conscious and deliberate effort on our part.

Being alert to the reality and presence of God in our personal world means learning how to pray. The most important element in prayer is an attitude of being attentive to the Lord. Like Elijah on Mount Horeb, we are surrounded by thunder, lightning and earthquake, but it is the "light silent sound" of God that we need to hear (1 Kings 19:11-12).

God is constantly whispering to us that we are his "little flock"—that we are precious in his eyes and that he wants very much to give us the freedom and joy of his kingdom. But too often we are not listening. We are bombarded by sounds and sights that frighten and confuse us. The only remedy is to attune our ears to the divine sounds of love and harmony and peace. We recall the words of the Book of Revelation: "Behold, I stand at the door and knock. If anyone hears my voice and opens the door, [then] I will enter his house and dine with him and he with me" (3:20). But we need to be quiet if we wish to hear the Lord knocking at the door of our hearts.

We all know how distressing it is to be saying something only to discover that no one is listening. At such times we realize that attentive listening is one of the most precious gifts that we can offer to another person. It is also a precious gift to God when we offer him our attentiveness. And when we do so, God will speak to us as he spoke to Jesus at his baptism: "You are my beloved child; in you I am well pleased." These words, spoken very softly, can change the world for us.

Demetrius R. Dumm, O.S.B.

Twentieth Sunday in Ordinary Time
Luke 12: 49-53

Gospel Summary

In this passage Jesus speaks of the meaning of his life. To fulfill his God-given destiny, he has resolutely set his face toward Jerusalem. There, refusing to be diverted from his mission of love, he will be rejected, suffer greatly and meet a violent death. He says that he is filled with great anguish until the mission he has been given is completed. Sensing a growing hostility, he tells his disciples that his intention is not to establish peace, but rather division--dividing even households and families.

Life Implications

At first glance one would not recognize the sayings of Jesus in this gospel passage as good news—there is the allusion to his own suffering and death, as well as his statement about bringing division, not peace. People in bondage to any kind of slavery or oppression, however, would have no trouble understanding exactly what Jesus is talking about. They would know that what they were hearing was good news. When someone like Martin Luther King appears in a situation where people are hopelessly caught in oppression, the immediate consequence is not peace, but division—even in households and families.

An oppressive system does not fix itself of its own accord. It takes a strong person of compassion not merely to lament injustice, but to risk life itself to proclaim liberation from oppression and hope of a new way of living. The very presence of such a person provokes a crisis whereby everyone involved in the system must choose either actively to hope for the new reality or to resist its coming.

Jesus understood that he had been sent to a fallen world in bondage—a humanity hopelessly mired in false value-systems of covetousness, violence, and idolatry. This was not merely some local situation of economic oppression imposed by a selfish landowner. Jesus was engaged in a cosmic struggle against the realm of Satan in order to restore God's kingdom to people long held in slavery to demonic powers. Paul, particularly in his Letter to the Romans, speaks of the universality of the bondage. All humanity lives under the power of sin. And even with the most well-intentioned effort, those in slavery—Jews and Gentiles alike—are not able to live according to God's will.

Jesus symbolically shows that he has entered the realm of Satan with God's power to liberate humanity from bondage by casting out demons. He shows that people will be able to use their freedom to live in a new way by curing people paralyzed to inaction by illness. Jesus in his own life shows what it means to be completely free from the false value-systems of Satan's reign, and to live in submission to God's reign—not as to a powerful king, but to a loving father.

As we hear the words of Jesus about the meaning of his life at our Eucharistic liturgy, we realize that they are living words spoken to us. Jesus means to provoke a crisis of decision in us even though it might disturb the peace and cause division. If we hear his words in faith, we will take a close look at the system of values whereby in practice we live our own lives. Though professing membership in the Church, am I still in bondage to the false value-systems of a fallen world? How do I define the meaning of my life? How do I define the meaning of success?

Jesus, now Risen Lord, is present among us not only to provoke a crisis of decision, but to enable us to actualize the reality of God's reign in ourselves. In that reality, although it may cost us something, we too can enter situations of oppression with the compassion and healing power of Jesus. With God's grace, we too can sometimes be instruments of liberation and hope for people who are held in bondage.

Campion P. Gavaler, O.S.B.

Twenty-first Sunday in Ordinary Time
Luke 13:22-30

Gospel Summary

Luke reminds us once again that we are on the "way to Jerusalem" with Jesus. This means that the guiding principle in our lives ought to be the loving concern that took Jesus himself to the climax of his career as he gave his life for us in Jerusalem. Though it would be nice if we could all visit the modern city of Jerusalem, this is not what Luke had in mind. He is thinking instead about the true purpose of this human life that God has given us.

As we make this spiritual journey, we must inevitably ask the question posed in today's gospel: "Lord, will only a few people be saved?" Or, more directly, "Lord, am I among those who will make this journey successfully?" And Jesus answers our question with words that dispel any smugness that we may have been entertaining: "Strive to enter through the narrow door." To love as he did will not be easy.

Finally, Jesus warns us about the terrible disappointment in store for those who have not taken his teaching seriously. They will discover, only when it is too late, that they have not made room in their lives for the One who alone can bring them to that ultimate joyful banquet that our Creator has prepared for us in his kingdom.

Life Implications

Most of us live in a world that is full of wonderful opportunities. A telling metaphor is the superabundance of our grocery stores. When we enter the supermarket, we scarcely know where to turn in view of all the delightful attractions that surround us. It has been noted that those who come here from impoverished countries are almost overwhelmed by amazement at the seemingly endless riches of these grocery stores.

We should all be grateful for such convenience in our lives, but we also know that such displays of worldly goods do not represent the real meaning of happiness. Some years ago, it was common to find contests offered on the radio with the winner awarded "20 minutes of free shopping in the supermarket." One can easily imagine the winner's frenetic search for the most desirable items. But I like to imagine a different scenario where the winning contestant would spend those precious minutes helping others with their shopping needs. And when questioned about this strange behavior, he would reply simply, "Oh, didn't you know that my Father owns the supermarket and that, if we are kind and thoughtful during our 20 minutes of life, the whole store will be ours forever?"

What a pity it will be if we finally see what life is all about only when it is too late! But there is still time to resist the powerful distractions that dazzle us and tell us how much more we need when only one thing is really necessary, that is, to love our gracious and generous God and to be kind and forgiving toward his precious people.

Demetrius R. Dumm, O.S.B.

Twenty-second Sunday in Ordinary Time
Luke 14:1,7-14

Gospel Summary

Jesus is having dinner at the home of one of the leading Pharisees, and people are observing him carefully. Noticing that the guests were choosing the places of honor at table, he tells a parable about the embarrassment suffered by a person who had chosen a place of honor and then was made to take the lowest place. Jesus then turns to the host and says to him: When you hold a dinner, don't invite those who can repay you; rather, invite the poor, the crippled, the lame, the blind because of their inability to repay you. If you do that, Jesus adds, you will be repaid at the resurrection of the righteous.

Life Implications

Jesus addresses both the guests invited to a banquet, and the host who does the inviting. At first glance, his suggestion to take the lowest place of honor when invited seems like a bit of human wisdom that might save someone a little embarrassment—hardly worth Luke's including it in his gospel. We are alerted, however, to a deeper meaning when we notice that Luke mentions that Jesus is telling us this as a parable. A parable surprises us with a meaning that is beyond the obvious, and upsets our usual way of thinking. The deeper dimension in this case is whether we have been exalting ourselves before God.

Jesus is not particularly concerned about the little embarrassment of having to take a lower place at a banquet. He is concerned about the possibility of a Big Embarrassment before the judgment of God—the host who has invited us to the banquet of life. Luke provides an illustration of what Jesus is talking about in the parable about the Pharisee and the tax collector (Luke 18:9-14). The tax collector, who would not even raise his eyes to heaven, went home justified rather than the Pharisee who had exalted himself before God.

What Jesus tells us about the way we extend hospitality is most radical in its life implications. The natural human tendency is to treat those people well who have or who will treat us well. There is nothing wrong with this sort of business deal—the world would not function very well unless we made business arrangements every day. Jesus, however, is talking about a divine kind of hospitality, and asks us to imitate him in that. Our generosity ought to be a characteristic of our personal freedom, not dependent on how people treat us. And besides, to attempt to determine who deserves our love implies a judgment of another person's soul that only God can make.

Again, Luke provides a good illustration of what Jesus is talking about in his parable about the Good Samaritan (Luke 10:25-37). A theologian asks Jesus, "And who is my neighbor?" Jesus responds by telling a parable about the Samaritan who showed mercy to a man in need: instead of trying to figure out who a deserving neighbor might be, one should become a neighbor by choosing to help those in need.

Graham Greene in his novel *The Power and the Glory* had a clear sense that the kind of love Jesus was talking about is the essence of divine love, and by grace a possibility of human love. The fugitive "whiskey priest" (realizing that the mestizo whom he had met would one day betray him) came to this awareness: "It was for this world Christ had died; the more evil you saw and heard about you, the greater glory lay around the death. It was too easy to die for what was good and beautiful...it needed God to die for the half-hearted and the corrupt."

When I taught Greene's novel in a first-year college religion class, I asked students if there is anyone for whom they would give their life—their mom, their dad, their brother, sister, friend? To do so certainly would be heroic, and would reflect the glory of divine love. Then I can see the incredulous negative look in their faces when I ask, "Would you give your life for Osama bin Laden?" Yet, it was for Osama bin Laden as well as for the rest of us—the undeserving world—that Christ gave his life. "But God proves his love for us in that while we were still sinners Christ died for us" (Romans 5:8).

Campion P. Gavaler, O.S.B.

Twenty-third Sunday in Ordinary Time
Luke 14:25-33

Gospel Summary

Luke was a native of the ancient city of Antioch in Syria. This was a major trading center where the inhabitants represented extremes of wealth and poverty—something that was unusual in Israel. The cold-hearted philosophy of power experienced by Luke in Antioch caused him to be overwhelmed by the contrasting tenderness of the all-powerful God of Israel. Hence his wonderful gospel stories about the mercy of God, e.g. the parable of the prodigal son.

This discovery of God's unconditional love and mercy caused Luke to insist also on the need to respond to that love in a similarly unconditional way. As this gospel passage makes clear, there can be no waffling or temporizing where commitment to Christ is concerned. Therefore, all other considerations, such as the claims of relatives, friends or possessions, must be subordinated to the absolute claim of God on those who have discovered his love and mercy.

We are often surprised and made uneasy by the rather shocking language Luke uses in reference to our relationship with family members. In that regard, it should be noted that "hating" in this context should simply be understood as the opposite of loving and would have the sense then of "not preferring." This is quite clear in the corresponding text in Matthew's gospel: "Whoever loves father or mother more than me is not worthy of me" (10:37).

Life Implications

To the extent that we have personally experienced the merciful love of God—something that may only gradually dawn on us—we should be ready and willing to commit ourselves, as much as humanly possible, to making that same unconditional love available to others. This means, among other things, that we will not ask in advance whether we think they deserve it. Their need should be the only real consideration. Luke reminds us that this will mean following the often painful path of the cross as we put the needs of others before our own wishes. All the while, we will need to keep the love and care of others central in our lives, even as we hear the siren song of the world, including at times the well-intentioned wishes of our own family and friends.

All of this is illustrated by Luke in the unmistakable analogies of a builder who must consider carefully the cost of his total project before he begins his work or of a king who must do the same before committing troops to battle. In other words, following Christ is serious business and demands resolute dedication. There is no place here for dilettantes or eclectics. We hear much today about "cafeteria Catholics" who pick and choose what they like in the teaching of Jesus and of the Church.

The danger here is that we are not naturally inclined to choose to be loving and caring in any absolute way but only in accordance with our personal preferences. In such a context, renouncing all our possessions for the sake of Christ does not mean becoming a beggar. It does mean, however, that we discover that our true identity will no longer be determined by social status but only by our personal and radical devotion to the wisdom of Jesus.

Those who try to live in this loving way will also learn how incredibly loving God can be.

Demetrius R. Dumm, O.S.B.

Twenty-fourth Sunday in Ordinary Time
Luke 15:1-32

Gospel Summary

The Pharisees and scribes are complaining that Jesus is a companion of tax collectors and sinners: "This man welcomes sinners and eats with them." Jesus responds to the criticism through three parables. In the first two parables, a shepherd's finding a lost sheep and a woman's finding a lost coin are compared to the joy of God upon finding a lost sinner. In the third parable, Jesus reveals that God is like a father who welcomes back a prodigal son who had left home and foolishly squandered his share of the estate. Furthermore, the father continues to love an older, resentful son who refuses to join in welcoming back his younger brother.

Life Implications

In the social-religious culture of that time, sinners and those in dishonorable occupations, as well as those who associated with them, were judged to be excluded from friendship with God. In the parables Jesus justifies his companionship with social and religious outcasts by implying that what he is doing reflects his knowledge of God's nature and God's will. In another place in Luke's gospel, Jesus' claim of acting with divine authority is made explicit: "No one knows who the Son is except the Father, and who the Father is except the Son and anyone to whom the Son wishes to reveal him" (10:22). (This central theme of the Son's knowledge of the Father is developed more theologically in the Last Supper Discourse of the Fourth Gospel.)

In the three parables of today's gospel Jesus reveals the joyful news that God loves us. There could be no deeper source of awareness of our worth than to trust Jesus and to believe that we human beings are truly precious in the eyes of God. Further life-implications may come to light if we imaginatively identify with the Pharisees and scribes to whom the parables are addressed and also with the two sons of the third parable.

We succumb to the self-righteous illusion of the Pharisees and scribes when we judge that some of our fellow human beings are excluded from God's love, and thereby may be excluded from our love. We become like the foolish younger son when we fall victim to the illusion that our happiness and freedom lie in autonomy from God. We become like the older son when we remain in our Father's house, but do not experience the joy of being at home. The older brother did not live as a child of a loving father, but as an employee who keeps track of what the boss owes to him and to other employees as well. In his resentment of unfair compensation, he can no longer recognize his brother as brother.

In Jesus' third parable, only the younger son comes to his senses and returns to his father, who forgetting his own dignity runs to welcome him home as a beloved child. If today we receive the grace to be freed from our own illusions, we can also come to identify with the attitude of Jesus and allow God's love to be present in the world through our actions. This is the most effective way of proclaiming to the world that God truly does love all of us as his own children.

Luke in his gospel repeatedly points out that Jesus sought to be in harmony with his Father's will through prayer. In this way he wants to teach us that only through prayer can we have confidence of acting in harmony with God's will in the particular circumstances of our lives. Also in prayer, we ask for the grace that will enable us to respond to new criticisms of God's ways with the insight and wit of Jesus.

Campion P. Gavaler, O.S.B.

Twenty-fifth Sunday in Ordinary Time
Luke 16:1-13

Gospel Summary

In order to appreciate fully the import of today's gospel text, which gives us the parable of the Unjust Steward, we must remember that parables, unlike allegories, focus on only one element in the comparison. Thus, the lesson to be drawn from this parable is that the followers of Jesus must also act prudently in regard to their own future prospects.

It should also be noted that this steward, though lacking in good management, was probably not as unjust as at first appears. In all likelihood, he was simply subtracting his own substantial commission from the debt owed to his master. This would be similar to the prudence of a small-market baseball team that trades away a good player because he is eligible for free agency and will be lost anyway!

The sayings that follow the parable sharpen its focus by making it clear that what Jesus has in mind is the attitude that his followers must adopt in regard to their earthly possessions, whether they be wealth or personal talents. If one allows these human and temporal things to monopolize one's attention, there is grave danger that the eternal treasure will be lost.

Life Implications

A distinctive feature of Luke's gospel is the deep concern he shows for the dangerous situation of wealthy or talented individuals who have become so engrossed in managing their riches that they are fatally distracted from the real purpose of human life. In this situation, they may very well be so distracted that they will discover, only when it is too late, that they have wasted the only ultimately significant opportunity in their lives. This same lesson is found in the situation of a strikingly beautiful person who has never needed to develop a mature and pleasing personality. This is what is meant when we speak of the "curse" of great talent.

This wisdom is also dramatically portrayed in Luke's parable of the rich man and Lazarus (16:19-31). It is important to notice that this rich man is never presented as one who has acquired his wealth through crime or some other immoral strategy. He ends up in hell simply because he is so preoccupied in managing his wealth that he does not notice that a poor man is starving on his doorstep!

This sensitivity of Luke concerning the danger of earthy possessions derives in part from his observation of the effect of wealth on the inhabitants of his hometown of Antioch. This was a prosperous trading center where the extremes of wealth and poverty were clearly evident. Luke warns, therefore, that possessions can have, in a sense, a drugging effect on their owners. One sees this clearly in Luke's story of the rich farmer who is worrying about building bigger barns for his bountiful harvest whereas God is calling him to face final judgment (12:16-20).

Luke does not condemn wealth as such. What he does condemn is a preoccupation or obsession with riches that precludes one's need to place the awareness of others and of their needs at the top of one's list of responsibilities. When the gospel says that we must choose between God and mammon, it is asking us to declare where we finally put our trust. Wealth and talents can serve God's purposes, but they must never replace God as the center of our attention in life.

Demetrius R. Dumm, O.S.B.

Twenty-sixth Sunday in Ordinary Time
Luke 16:19-31

Gospel Summary

Today's gospel passage contains Jesus' story about a rich man who dined sumptuously each day and Lazarus, a poor man, who would gladly have eaten the scraps from the rich man's table. When the poor man died, angels carried him to the bosom of Abraham. When the rich man died, he found himself in the netherworld of torment. He was, however, able to see Abraham with Lazarus in a place of honor at his side. The rich man asked Abraham to send Lazarus so that he might give him a drop of water to relieve his suffering. Abraham replied that this was no longer a possibility.

The rich man then asked Abraham to send Lazarus to his five brothers so that he might warn them, lest they suffer the same torment that had befallen him. Abraham replied "They have Moses and the prophets. Let them listen to them." The rich man said that his brothers would repent if someone from the dead warned them. Abraham responded that if they do not listen to Moses and the prophets, they would not be persuaded even if someone should rise from the dead.

Life Implications

One of the striking things about parables is that they often overturn conventional ways of thinking. If we are able to hear them with grace, they can shock us out of the illusions that we are accustomed to live by, and enable us to see things with God's eyes. In regard to the scene of today's gospel, our way of looking at things is not much different from the way people of Jesus' culture looked at things. If we see a rich man and a poor man, our envy would be in the direction of the rich man. Further, we would have the feeling, perhaps unspoken, that the poor man's miserable condition was probably a consequence of his own laziness or irresponsible action. Yet, in this story the rich man is surely not the one to be envied. What's going on here?

At the end of the story, we feel bad that Lazarus is not able to warn the rich man's five brothers. But the parable tricks us. We, all of us, are the five brothers or the five sisters. And it is the rich man, himself, who is able to warn us. It isn't difficult to imagine the sort of things he wants to say.

This will be the rich man speaking. There is finality to life and to life's choices. Don't be in the illusion of imagining the end of your life to be something like the end of the cosmos—far in the distant future. God may say to you: "You fool, this night your life will be demanded of you." The choices you are making now have everlasting consequences. You, as I once did, have the power to establish a chasm between yourself and the Lazarus lying at your door. After you die, that chasm is forever fixed; and you will no longer be able to cross it.

I want to warn you especially about riches, riches of all kinds—of money, intelligence, health, power, social or religious status. Though all good in themselves, these riches can lead you to forget about God and everyone else except yourself. That's what happened to me. And most people, including myself, thought I was a big success in life. Remember that God identifies with every Lazarus of the world—the hungry, the thirsty, the sick, the unborn, even criminals in prison. One of them is lying at your door. If you establish a chasm between Lazarus and yourself, you are establishing a chasm between yourself and God.

That ends the rich man's warning to us. But after all, the rich man is only a fictional character in a story Jesus made up for simple folk of a pre-scientific age. Does it any longer have meaning for us? To decide that question will be the most important decision we will ever make. Do I trust that Jesus is alive and present among us to tell me how God sees things, or do I listen to other, much louder voices that promise me more money, more knowledge, more health, more power, higher social or religious status? This homily, like most others, must end with a prayer: Lord, I believe. Help my unbelief. You have the words of everlasting life.

Campion P. Gavaler, O.S.B.

Twenty-seventh Sunday in Ordinary Time
Luke 17:5-10

Gospel Summary:

Luke is still leading us toward Jerusalem, the place where we turn everything over to God. In the verses that precede today's gospel passage, Jesus has challenged his disciples to forgive offenders as many as seven times each day. This seems almost impossible and so the disciples ask Jesus to increase their faith, i.e. to give them the courage and the strength needed to live according to such high ideals.

Jesus agrees that their faith must grow and, when he says that real faith could cause a mulberry tree to be transplanted into the sea, he is using a metaphor to tell them how radically their lives would change if they would only allow him to fill them with his own vision of life. Moving a mulberry tree would be nothing compared to the radical transformation of the landscape of their lives that would come from generous faith.

The story that follows about a servant who should not expect special recognition just because he has done his duty illustrates in a very graphic way some consequences that flow from this radically new faith vision that should be characteristic of our daily lives.

Life Implications:

It is a little disconcerting to hear Jesus telling the servants who have done their duty that they are to consider themselves "unprofitable." Most translations falter here. The Greek original suggests simply that these servants should not expect anything further, i.e. that they should not be looking for special attention or approval.

In the context, this means that their faith has proven deficient. If they had real faith, they would be so confident and joyful that they would not need to be looking constantly for approval and reassurance of their worth. Their confidence would come from the love of God that they experience to the extent that they no longer need to be stroked or coddled as if job-approval was all that mattered in life. This does not mean that one should be careless about the quality of one's work, but it does mean that the only ultimately satisfying approval comes from the sure experience of God's loving presence.

There is a lesson here also for those who are especially needy, such as the sick or disabled. They certainly deserve our personal, loving attention and care, but they too, like the "unprofitable servants," can sometimes be more demanding and ungrateful than their condition warrants.

St. Benedict, who was a wise observer of human foibles, offers sound advice in this regard: "Let the sick...bear in mind that they are served out of honor for God, and let them not by their excessive demands distress their brothers who serve them." The key is to be in touch with God and then it will not be necessary to play the victim, whether one is an "unappreciated" servant or an unhappy patient.

Caregivers are often required to have almost heroic patience in their work. I have often thought that they should try to understand that their cranky patients are probably angry with God and not with them. These patients are still struggling to accept what has happened to them and we should not take their resistance too personally. After all, it takes time to realize that God's love is sometimes expressed in ways we do not understand.

Demetrius R. Dumm, O.S.B.

Twenty-eighth Sunday in Ordinary Time
Luke 17:11-19

Gospel Summary

Jesus, continuing his journey to Jerusalem, comes upon ten lepers, and from a distance hears their plea for help, "Jesus, Master! Have pity on us!" He instructs these outcastes from society to go and show themselves to the priests. On the way, they are cleansed of their leprosy. One of them, a Samaritan, returns glorifying God, and falls at the feet of Jesus in gratitude. Jesus remarks, "Has none but this foreigner returned to give thanks to God?" Then to the Samaritan, "Stand up and go; your faith has saved you."

Life Implications

As always in the teaching of Jesus, it is faith that will determine whether we identify with the nine who are cured but not saved, or with the Samaritan who is both cured and saved. All ten lepers are healed. They all experience their return to health and to membership in the community as a good thing. However, only the Samaritan, with the intuition of faith, recognizes the good thing to be a gift of God, and acts upon that intuition. He glorifies God, and returns to thank Jesus whom he recognizes as an agent of God's presence and compassion.

In the language of later theology, the Samaritan's faith enabled him to see with sacramental vision. Without the vision of faith, one can experience countless good things—the wonders of the universe through the eyes of science; the ability to hear, to see, to speak, to feel; a return to health from an illness. But it is only with the intuition of faith that one can experience these good things as gifts of God. Through faith they become symbols or sacraments of the personal exchange of love—God's self-giving to us, and our grateful response in word and deed. Because the Samaritan entered into that personal exchange of divine love and human gratitude, Jesus said to him, "Stand up and go; your faith has saved you." To possess health, or for that matter any other good thing of this earth, in the judgment of Jesus is not to be saved.

Faith of course must not be restricted to recognizing a good thing as God's gift only in the miracle moments of life. Rather, as Saint Paul tells us, faith means to live in the awareness of the divine presence as a way of life, "giving thanks always and for everything in the name of our Lord Jesus Christ to God the Father" (Eph 5:20). My favorite part of the *Talmud* ("Berakhot") illustrates this essential aspect of the biblical tradition by giving examples when a faithful person will bless God in gratitude: "on seeing the ocean, on seeing the first tree blossom in the spring, on seeing a friend after six months, on hearing a sage, on receiving good news, on receiving bad news."

Each Sunday, like the Samaritan, we return to celebrate the Eucharist in gratitude for all the gifts that God has showered upon us as individuals and as a community. With a sacramental vision of faith, we hear the words of the bible as the gift of God's Word to us; we believe that the people around us are the church, the Body of Christ; we affirm the bread and wine truly to be the Risen Lord, the Father's ultimate gift to us. And with hearts lifted up in faith we can pray, "Father, all-powerful and ever-living God, we do well always and everywhere to give you thanks through Jesus Christ our Lord."

Campion P. Gavaler, O.S.B.

Twenty-ninth Sunday in Ordinary Time
Luke 18: 1-8

Gospel Summary:

The classic way to stay in touch with God is prayer. Small wonder then that Luke writes so insistently about prayer when he shows us how to accompany Jesus on his journey to Jerusalem. Although the ideal prayer for Christians is praise and thanksgiving, there is also a place for prayers of petition, as today's gospel parable makes quite clear.

The story-line of the parable is clear and compelling. In ancient Israel, widows were often listed among the more vulnerable members of society. And it appears that the widow of the parable has in fact been defrauded of her property by unscrupulous persons. Her only recourse is the local judge. But he has long since abandoned his covenant morality and is swayed only by bribes—something that the destitute widow cannot provide.

This unprincipled judge is proud of his freedom from the demands of true religion, Moreover, he is happy to proclaim this false freedom on every occasion. (He may remind us of the agnostic physician in Bernanos' *Diary of a Country Priest*). However, the persistence of the widow gradually wears him down and finally causes him to grant her justice. The lesson drawn by Jesus is crystal clear: How much more likely is God, the most just of all judges, ready to grant our requests for justice when we are treated unfairly!

Life Implications:

The point of this parable is probably more subtle than we may at first surmise. Jesus is not just telling us that we must doggedly persevere in prayer even when no answer seems to be provided. That is true, no doubt, but the real point here concerns our attitude toward God. For many of us, God seems so remote and so insensitive to our pleas that we may feel that he is not that different from the judge in the parable. As a matter of experience, our God does not always seem ready to give us the justice that we seek.

The deeper lesson of the parable is concerned, therefore, with our experience of the reality and presence of God in our lives. It is faith alone that enables us to experience God as One who is exceedingly good and who loves us very much. We will want to persist in our prayers to him, not just because we need his help, but primarily because we want simply to stay in touch with this wonderful Person, who loves us unconditionally. In the long run, this loving God will give us all that we need...and much more.

Our relationship with God is not unlike that of children who expect their parents to respond positively to every request they have. But good and loving parents know that these requests are not always in the best interest of their children. I suspect that many children would quit school or eat only junk food if their parents would allow it. The important thing for all concerned is to maintain a loving and trusting contact, in spite of occasional bumps in the road. Today's parable reminds us that this is even more true of our relationship with God.

Demetrius R. Dumm, O.S.B.

Thirtieth Sunday in Ordinary Time
Luke 18:9-14

Gospel Summary

Luke introduces the parable about a Pharisee and a tax collector with the statement that it is addressed "to those who were convinced of their own righteousness and despised everyone else." Two men go up to the temple to pray. The Pharisee, standing in a prominent place, thanks God that he is not like the rest of humanity—or even like the tax collector he had noticed. He also reminds God that he fasts twice a week, and pays tithes on his whole income. The tax collector, standing at a distance, beats his breast and prays, "O God, be merciful to me a sinner." Jesus then remarks that the tax collector who humbled himself before God went home justified, not the Pharisee who had exalted himself.

Life Implications

Jesus chose to make the Pharisee a principal character of his parable because Pharisees were the most highly respected religious group in the community. Pharisees were intensely committed to the religious traditions of the people. They refused any collaboration with the occupying Roman military power. They kept the commandments, voluntarily fasted beyond the obligatory annual day of fasting, and even cut down on their standard of living to support the needs of the temple.

Jesus chose a tax collector as the opposite principal character because tax collectors were generally held in contempt by the people. They were not only collaborators with the hated Roman oppressors, but by collecting funds to support a corrupt imperial system, made it impossible for many people to fulfill their financial obligations to the temple. These petty government officials were adept at defrauding people by various strong-arm methods, and were regarded as no better than robbers.

The Pharisee of the parable had every good reason to thank God for the worthiness of his own life, and to despise the tax collector as one who was a threat not only to the temple, but to everything that was worthwhile and holy. When Jesus at the conclusion of his parable remarked that the tax collector went home justified, not the Pharisee, it must have seemed like a shockingly unfair conclusion. He had taken the risk of pressing the parable to the edge of unfairness in order to teach something essential about the way we stand with God.

Jesus in his parable obviously is not advocating collaboration with an oppressive military power, cheating people, moral relativism, or much less, forbidding evaluation of evil behavior or false teaching. The Pharisee is condemned because he assumed God's role in judging the spiritual worth of a fellow human being. He exalted himself above the rest of humanity, and despised another through the comparisons he fashioned in his prayer.

It is incidental whether the Pharisee or the tax collector is the one who exalts himself in the sight of God. In today's culture, Jesus would probably have someone like the tax collector exalt himself and despise others in his prayer: "O God, I thank you that I am not like the rest of humanity—greedy, dishonest, adulterous—or even like this tax collector." The desire to exalt oneself can always find a reason—even one's humility.

Today at our Eucharist we ask to be freed from illusions that we have fashioned about ourselves, and pray for the grace of sharing in Christ's humility. Through his authentic humility, we will be able to stand before God in our own unique truth, and thus make it possible to receive divine mercy and go home justified.

Campion P. Gavaler, O.S.B.

Thirty-first Sunday in Ordinary Time
Luke 19:1-10

Gospel Summary

Jesus has now arrived at Jericho and so his long journey to Jerusalem is almost over. He has been modeling for us our own journey of faith. When he meets Zachaeus he reminds us that it will not be possible to go with him all the way to Cross and Resurrection without total generosity.

In the previous chapter, the rich ruler cannot abandon his wealth in order to follow Jesus (18:18). By contrast, Zachaeus is happy to share half of his possessions with the poor. The wealthy ruler appears to be pious and observant, whereas Zachaeus has been collecting taxes for the hated Roman occupiers of his country. Nonetheless, he is the one who is looking for Jesus and he is the one with whom Jesus wishes to be associated.

Much has been made of the fact that Zachaeus was "short of stature," so that he had to climb a sycamore tree in order to see, and be seen by, Jesus. Today we would say that he was a little man with a big heart!

Life Implications

The gospel tells us that Zachaeus was a rich man. We may assume, therefore, that he was not like most of us, who would no doubt be surprised if someone should call us rich. In fact, we are wealthy in many ways that do not involve money, such as talent, kindness or sensitivity. And so we need to ask ourselves whether we are as generous as was Zachaeus in sharing our own gifts. Do we think that much about the poor? Do we realize that the "poor" are often those who need a kind word or a friendly smile?

This gospel story reminds us also that we must be very careful not to judge others because of their appearance. We are told that those who accompanied Jesus began to grumble when he chose to be a guest of this marginal Jew, who seemed to be collaborating with the Romans. But, as a matter of fact, this was one of those jobs that someone had to do. The real world is not as neat as we might like it to be. The point is that Zachaeus "redeemed" his unsavory work by the generosity that he brought to it.

It should also be noted that Zachaeus did not live in the illusion of self-sufficiency. He knew that somehow his life was incomplete without Jesus. And he did not allow his short stature to become an excuse for not seeking Jesus. Nor did Jesus consider his "inadequacy" to be an obstacle. Jesus wants to be a guest in all our homes. Our desire to welcome him will easily cancel any feelings of unworthiness that may hold us back. The kindness we offer to others can more than make up any "shortness" we may have.

Demetrius R. Dumm, O.S.B.

Thirty-second Sunday in Ordinary Time

Luke 20:27-38

Gospel Summary

Some Sadducees, denying belief in resurrection, pose a hypothetical question to Jesus about seven brothers who, after each other's death, marry the same woman. The Sadducees ask whose wife that woman will be at the resurrection. Jesus replies that those who are deemed worthy to share to the resurrection of the dead are not married to anyone. They can no longer die, and they themselves are all children of God. Then Jesus points out that the Sadducees should know this from the passage in Exodus where God appears to Moses in the burning bush. The Lord said to Moses, "I am the God ... of Abraham, the God of Isaac, and the God of Jacob." It is evident, Jesus says, that the Lord is "not God of the dead, but of the living; for to him all are alive.""

Life Implications

In Luke's gospel, Jesus seems quite reticent in talking at length about the specifics of life after death. To the Sadducees' question, Jesus simply replies that after resurrection there will no longer be a need of bearing children—we will all be children of God. In other episodes of the gospel there is the same reticence. Jesus alludes to gaining a reward in heaven and the coming of the Son of Man in glory. Lazarus in a parable will be carried by angels to the bosom of Abraham. In his last hour, Jesus promises Paradise to the thief who is dying with him on a cross. The principal focus, however, of Jesus' teaching is on the present. "Blessed are those who hear the word of God and observe it" (Luke 11:28). They will be counted among the blessed at the Lord's coming in judgment.

Jesus' attention to the supreme importance of responding to the reality of the present moment is evident not only in his teaching, but in his own life. Luke tells us that when Jesus realized that his own death was imminent, he did not explain to his disciples what would happen to him after his death. Rather, he prayed, "Father, if you are willing, take this cup away from me; still, not my will but yours be done" (Luke 22: 42). It is in the reality of that moment that Jesus hears the word of God, and keeps it. He could put his life into God's hands at that moment because he trusted that the God of Abraham, Isaac, and Jacob would not abandon him to the power of death.

We encounter God and can respond to his will only in the narrow gate of our own present moment, our day of salvation. We do not encounter God in the feelings of past moments that we try to hang on to, or in the feelings of future moments that we try to imagine. Now is the only time for the decision of faith and for the works of love.

Because God is the God of the living, when we encounter God in faith we are in the presence of all who are in communion with God. Each Sunday in the Eucharistic Prayer, we sing "Holy, Holy, Holy" with the Risen Lord and with all who are alive in him. It is a natural trajectory from the good news of Jesus' affirmation that our life as God's children does not end with death to the good news that Pope Paul VI gave us to affirm in the Credo of the People of God. "We believe in the communion of all the faithful of Christ, those who are pilgrims on earth, the dead who are being purified, and the blessed in heaven, all together forming one church; and we believe that in this communion, the merciful love of God and his saints is always attentive to our prayers."

Campion P. Gavaler, O.S.B.

Thirty-third Sunday in Ordinary Time

Luke 21:5-19

Gospel Summary

It has been traditional to reflect on an end-of-the-world gospel passage as we approach the end of the liturgical year. We will also be offered a similar gospel passage on the First Sunday of Advent. It is important to note this because, from a biblical perspective, the end of one world is not such a tragic event since it also announces the beginning of a new one. A sorrowful 'Good-bye' must sometimes be accepted before there can be a joyous 'Hello!'

We should note that in today's gospel the end of the world is presented on various levels. The immediate end is the chaotic and painful experience that came when the Romans destroyed the Jewish temple. For Christians at least, this represented the end of the Old Testament era. Secondly, there are hints also of the final, cosmic end of our world with falling stars and dimming of the sun and moon. Finally, in both of these endings we see the elements of the end of our own earthly world in the event we call death.

The phenomena that accompany the final, cosmic end are surprisingly similar to the experiences that often come with our own last days. The failure of the sun and moon and the erratic behavior of the stars are replicated among us when we lose the security represented by these usually reliable heavenly bodies. For instance, when we grow old we sometimes find it hard to remember what time of the day it is. But this is only the end of a world that was never meant to last. We hate to see it go, but God knows what is best for us.

Life Implications

When we try to understand the gospel passages concerning the end of the world, it may be helpful to compare this event with human birth, which, for the infant being born, must surely be a traumatic experience. In fact, if an infant were able to choose, I suspect that it would opt for a continued existence in the warm, safe womb of its mother. The infant does not yet know how tragic it would be to miss all the possibilities of independent human life.

We too live in this world in a kind of womb that is meant to prepare us for birth into a new and better existence. Unlike the infant, however, we can resist that birth and we may even see it as a kind of personal tragedy. If our faith were as strong and vital as it should be, this would not be the case. Instead, we would embrace our present life with gratitude and still be ready to leave it with grace and peace, as we welcome the homecoming that God keeps in store for his beloved children.

But we don't have to wait until death to begin living by the wisdom of the Bible. In our lives there are little worlds ending all the time—the end of childhood, of education, of employment, of strength, etc. The courage and generosity and trust with which we deal with these endings will prepare us for the final ending.

It is also true that every time we love unselfishly we die a little bit to our own precious plans and preferences. If we die daily in these small ways, we will have little difficulty with the final dying as our plans are once again revised and we offer our lives, once and for all, to a merciful and loving God.

A confrere, in a pensive mood, said to me one time that it didn't seem fair for God to give me life without consulting me and then to allow me to make a mess of it. I thought about that and concluded that the baptismal experience, as one begins to see its implications, is that incredible opportunity to agree with my Creator, that life is always a wonderful gift and we should be saying continuously: "Thank you, dear Lord!"

Demetrius R. Dumm, O.S.B.

Solemnities of the Lord During Ordinary Time

Feast of Christ the King, Cycle C
Luke 23:35-43

Gospel Summary

After his arrest, Jesus has been accused before Pilate, the Roman governor, of being opposed to Caesar and of claiming to be the Messiah of God, a king. Now, having been condemned to death under Roman law, Jesus is being crucified along with two criminals. The rulers and the soldiers taunt Jesus and call out that if he is the Messiah and king of the Jews, he should be able to save himself. One of the criminals also reviles Jesus saying, "Are you not the Messiah? Save yourself and us." The other criminal, however, recognizing his own crimes and the goodness of Jesus, says, "Jesus, remember me when you come into your kingdom." Jesus responds, "Amen, I say to you, today you will be with me in Paradise."

Life Implications

The rulers, soldiers, and the criminal who taunted Jesus had a definite notion of what it would mean if Jesus had been anointed by God as king. In their minds it would mean that Jesus would be a ruler of an empire—certainly more powerful than Caesar, and most certainly not a helpless victim of Caesar's power. We too may fall into the trap of projecting our own notions of what it means to honor Jesus as our king. Instead of projecting our own expectations, we must reflect on how Jesus reveals the meaning of authority in the kingdom he came to establish on earth.

Pope Pius XI, in his 1925 encyclical *Quas Primas* establishing the feast of Christ the King, reminds us of key texts for us to reflect upon today. In response to his disciples who were coveting positions of power, Jesus said that those who are rulers over the Gentiles make their authority over them felt. In his kingdom, however, whoever wishes to be great must be a servant, for he tells them that he himself "did not come to be served but to serve and to give his life as a ransom for many" (Mk 10:35-45). To Jesus, the king anointed by God, all power in heaven and on earth was given; yet he issued no imperial decree to be enforced by the power of the sword. Rather he said to all who would listen, "Come to me, all you who labor and are burdened, and I will give you rest. Take my yoke upon you and learn from me, for I am meek and humble of heart" (Mt 11:28-29). This is a king?

It is on the cross that Jesus ultimately reveals what it means to be king. The supreme power and glory of God that Jesus reveals is love. And in a world under Satan's reign of evil violence, it must be crucified love. Even though he challenges us to become engaged in the struggle to establish Christ's kingdom of justice and peace on earth, Pius XI calls us to a choice even more fundamental. In his encyclical, the Pope connects the feast of Christ the King to the feast of the Sacred Heart of Jesus. As king, Jesus gave his heart to us. "Lifted high on the cross, Christ gave his life for us, so much did he love us" (Preface for the feast of the Sacred Heart). He did so asking that we give our hearts to him.

At our Eucharist today we pray that each of us may truly believe that Jesus "the Son of God has loved me and given himself up for me" (Gal 2:20). And we ask for the grace to respond to this supreme love by giving ourselves and entrusting our lives to his reign. Perhaps for many of us, we may only be able to repeat the words of the criminal dying on his own cross: "Jesus, remember me when you come into your kingdom."

Campion P. Gavaler, O.S.B.

Trinity Sunday, Cycle C
John 16:12-15

Gospel Summary

In this passage from the Last Supper Discourse, Jesus tells his disciples that when the Spirit of Truth comes he will guide them in all truth. He then reveals the true nature of God as a communion of love. Everything the Father has he gives to the Son. Everything the Son has he gives to the Spirit. Everything the Spirit receives he gives to us. Thus the supreme mystery of the gospel: we human beings are offered the gift of living in the communion of eternal truth and love with the Father, Son, and Holy Spirit.

Life Implications

The structure of the Eucharistic liturgy that we celebrate enables us to express our faith that our true life even now is communion with the life of God. Each Sunday's gospel unfolds the mystery of the gift of divine life to us. In each gospel Jesus makes all that he receives from the Father's love visible and a gift to us through the power of the Holy Spirit.

In the Eucharistic Prayer that follows the proclamation of the gospel and homily, we lift up our hearts to be in union with the love of Christ and pray: "Through him, with him, in him, in the unity of the Holy Spirit, all glory and honor is yours, almighty Father, for ever and ever." When, with all the angels and saints, we have said "Amen" to entire church's prayer of gratitude, we ask our Father for the supreme gift of the Bread of Life. In receiving this Bread, which is the Lord, we enter into deeper communion of divine life. And we commit ourselves to allow all that we receive—the truth and the love—to flow through us to everyone we encounter in the circumstances of our lives.

Trinity Sunday is a good opportunity to pay special attention to what we do and pray every Sunday at Mass so that we realize more deeply that every Sunday is Trinity Sunday. In addition, the first Scripture reading (Proverbs 8:22-31) reminds us of the first affirmation of the creed that we proclaim every Sunday. Always and everywhere we ought to give thanks for the marvels of creation—gift of the Father to us through his eternal Divine Wisdom, the Word Incarnate.

We should not allow Trinity Sunday to pass by without mentioning the church's sacramentals, which remind us of our life in the trinity of divine love. One of my favorites is the famous Russian icon painted by Andrei Rublev in the early part of the fifteenth century. The three persons of the Holy Trinity—Rublev uses the image of the three angels who came to Abraham and Sarah in Genesis 18—sit at the eucharistic table in the unity of an intimately related half-circle, beckoning to be completed. The icon reveals that we are all invited to accept the hospitality of the three divine persons in their eternal home, and to share their gift of holy bread and wine.

Rublev's Holy Trinity icon reveals the deepest meaning of the mystery of the church as the communion of life with Father, Son, and Holy Spirit around the Eucharistic table of love. The tree of Mamre by which the Lord appeared to Abraham and Sarah is in the background of the icon. It calls to mind the tree in the middle of the Garden of Eden, and also the tree of the cross—the ultimate revelation of divine self-giving love made present for us in the Eucharist. The icon reveals the highest ideal and challenge of human existence. We are called to reflect in the church, in our families, and in our world the communion of love, which is the true nature of God. This is the glory and the joy for which we are created.

Campion P. Gavaler, O.S.B.

Feast of the Body and Blood of Christ, Cycle C
Luke 9:11b-17

Gospel Summary

Today's gospel passage is Luke's version of Jesus' miracle of the multiplication of loaves and fish. This is one of the most significant miracles of Jesus as is evident from the fact that it appears in all four gospels. The scenario is quite familiar: there is a large, hungry crowd; the disciples bring this to the attention of Jesus; he instructs them, almost casually, to provide food for them; the disciples protest that this is clearly impossible since they have scarcely enough for themselves.

In spite of their reservations, the disciples obey Jesus when, having blest the loaves and fish, he asks them to distribute them to the hungry crowd. To their total amazement, there is not only enough for all those present, but twelve baskets filled with fragments are left over.

We can easily understand why the Church has chosen this gospel story for the feast of the Body and Blood of Christ, for the primary theme of this feast is the nourishment that Jesus offers us in the Blessed Sacrament. We are now the hungry multitude and we are reminded that Jesus offers us a nourishment that fully satisfies our needs. This is so because the food he offers is his own life, given for us.

Life Implications

There is obviously something miraculous about the way in which Jesus solves the problem of the hungry multitude. We should admire that and see it as a sign of the concern and generosity of Jesus. But we should also remember that all the miracles of Jesus' early ministry were intended to show that he was approved by God and that his message should be trusted. After all, those whom Jesus fed or cured all got hungry or sick again and died. These miracles do not constitute salvation; they are simply the introduction of the Savior.

There is, however, an even more important lesson here. We can readily identify with the disciples as we face overwhelming problems in our own world. There is so much violence and injustice that we often feel paralyzed by the enormity of the challenge. Like the disciples, we feel that we have meager resources for dealing with these problems. Nonetheless, Jesus tells us also to take what little we have and to do what we can with it. There is an implied promise that God will join us and turn our "five loaves and two fish" into food for the multitude...with an abundance left over!

As we celebrate the Eucharist, we find again a super abundance that can nourish us in spite of great need. In the Mass, Jesus offers himself under the appearance of a few small wafers and a few drops of wine in a way that can nourish the whole world. Those of us who share in this divine meal should not only feel wonderfully nourished ourselves but also empowered to share our good fortune with all the hungry people whom we meet. No matter how poor we think we are, we become rich, for ourselves and for others, when we receive the boundless gift of God's love in the Eucharistic banquet.

Demetrius R. Dumm, O.S.B.

Feasts of Mary and Saints

Solemnity of the Immaculate Conception
Luke 1: 26–38

Gospel Summary:

Theologians often make a distinction between "high" Christology, which emphasizes the divine nature of Jesus, and "low" Christology, which emphasizes his human nature. This distinction finds a parallel in the case of Mary. Today's feast would belong to "high" Mariology, because it celebrates a special privilege of Mary which flows from her status as Mother of God. Most New Testament references to Mary, however, belong to "low" Mariology because they begin with a very human Mary responding to the initiative of the angel Gabriel.

This does not in any way detract from the importance of the Immaculate Conception of Mary, which celebrates the fact that she was without sin from the first moment of her conception. However, it does remind us that this wonderful privilege was granted to her by anticipation of her future status as mother of Jesus and, therefore, of God.

It is important to note that, as today's gospel makes clear, Mary's status as mother of God presupposes her response to the angel Gabriel with that magnificent expression of love and trust and generosity: "Behold, I am the handmaid of the Lord. May it be done to me according to your word" (Luke 1: 38). All the privileges of Mary derive from this moment of unconditional self-surrender to the plans of God. It should not surprise us, therefore, to see that the gospel of Luke devotes more attention to the Annunciation than to any other event of Mary's life.

Life Implications:

The sinless condition of Mary, from the beginning to the end of her life, elicits our admiration and prompts us to be grateful to God for making this possible in one who shares our nature as human beings. Although we certainly cannot imitate her sinless condition, we can be greatly encouraged by this signal victory over evil. We live in a world of so much sin and violence that we are tempted to wonder whether the light really can overcome the darkness, as John's Prologue promises (John 1: 5). But we are immensely reassured as we celebrate each year this victory of Mary, "our tainted nature's solitary boast" (William Wordsworth).

At the same time, we need to remember that this victory came directly from the willingness of Mary to accept a mysterious mission from God which, as she surely must have suspected, would lead to grievous suffering. We too need to make difficult choices that may demand much love and courage. And we too are aware that it may be very painful to remain faithful to the choices that God expects of us. In such situations, the generosity of Mary remains a wonderful model for us. Moreover, we can be sure that her maternal solicitude will accompany us as we try to live in accordance with our best instincts.

When we reflect upon the fact that sin is the worst kind of bondage, the sinless Mary is recognized also as the only one among us human beings who is truly free. Those who aspire to freedom solely through the acquisition of power should pause to consider that the ultimate freedom of Mary came through her resolute and loving obedience to the mission that God offered to her. She became a model of freedom through her loving generosity, and this will always be the only truly effective way to acquire human freedom and dignity.

Demetrius R. Dumm, O.S.B.

Solemnity of Mary Mother of God
Luke 2: 16–21

Gospel Summary

Today's gospel text suffers somewhat from being removed from its biblical context. We are told that the shepherds "went with haste and found Mary and Joseph, and the infant lying in the manger." It is helpful to note that they did this only because they had received a vision of angels who told them, "This will be a sign for you: you will find an infant wrapped in swaddling clothes and lying in a manger" (Luke 2: 12). The shepherds are thus taken out of their workaday worlds and asked to see their lives in a new and wonderful way.

The insistence on the image of an "infant wrapped in swaddling clothes," that is, wrapped in warm flannel, alerts us to a profound symbolism here, for the flannel bands stand for God's loving care which is shown to us in the coming of Jesus as our Savior. In a very real sense, we can say that God has wrapped the whole world in secure and loving bands by sending his beloved Son to us as an embodiment of endless loving kindness.

Since this feast is the feast of "Mary Mother of God," it is important to note also that "Mary kept all these things, reflecting on them in her heart." We are not told what "all these things" might be, but we can rest assured that they embraced the whole wonderful experience of bearing a child who is already destined to change the course of human history in ways that will be revealed only later—ways that will involve both painful self-sacrifice and glorious victory.

Life Implications

The beginning of a new year provides us with an opportunity to reflect on the special gift of time. We recall the events of the previous year and express our gratitude for all the good things that have happened, all the while being aware that there have also been sad and painful and perhaps sinful realities. But most of all we celebrate the promise of a new set of months and we try to be hopeful in spite of threats of war and recession and just growing older.

Today's gospel has a special message for us as we hang up the new calendar with mixed feelings. The fresh new year is in some ways like the infant Jesus "wrapped in swaddling clothes and lying in a manger." Both the new year and the new child seem so vulnerable, but the almighty power of God is hidden in the new year, just as it is in the tiny infant. God is fully prepared to wrap our fragile lives and hopes in the warm blanket of his ever-present and constant love. With such assurance, we can face the future with generous hope and with light hearts. For we too need to realize that the angels who spoke to the shepherds are speaking to us also when they say, "This will be a sign for you: you will find an infant wrapped in swaddling clothes and lying in a manger." Come, let us adore him.

Demetrius R. Dumm, O.S.B.

Saints Peter and Paul, Apostles
Matthew 16: 13–19

Gospel Summary

In his gospel Matthew establishes an inseparable link between the identity of Jesus and the meaning of the church. Further, Matthew affirms that the identity of Jesus and the meaning of the church are inseparable from the action of the heavenly Father. Simon from a revelation of the heavenly Father, not from flesh and blood, confesses Jesus to be "the Messiah, the Son of the living God." In response, Jesus confers upon Simon a new title, the Rock. Upon Simon, the Rock, Jesus, the Christ, promises to build his church. The gates of hell, Jesus further promises, shall not prevail against it. And to Simon Peter (from petra, the Greek word for "rock"), Jesus gives the keys to the kingdom of heaven with authority to "bind and loose" with divine sanction in the universal church (my church). On this feast of Peter and Paul, one should note Paul's affirmation that the heavenly Father, not flesh and blood, also revealed Jesus as Son to him (Galatians 1: 16).

Life Implications

In order to appreciate the lasting significance of the saints in the Catholic faith-tradition, we have to see the saints in relation to Christ, and thereby in relation to the Father and the Holy Spirit. It is through the creative action of the Spirit that we can see the saints as members of the church in divine-human personal communion. In this context we can then look at the unique personalities of the saints and examine their unique roles in actualizing Christ's mission in the world.

Peter certainly has both a unique personality and a unique role in actualizing Christ's mission in the world. Christ gives him his role as the solid Rock upon which he will build his church. However, Christ also calls him a rock that might cause him to stumble. By trying to talk Jesus out of following his heavenly Father's will, Peter becomes an agent of Satan (Matthew 16: 21–23). It is no surprise that history teaches us that this characterization of Jesus applies not only to Peter, but to Peter's successors as well. Christ continues to build his church upon the popes, Peter's successors as bishops of Rome; but like Peter they too at times can be like rocks on the road. Christ, however, does not permit evil to prevail over his church despite our human failings.

The gospels make no attempt to whitewash Peter's failures: he boasted about his loyalty to Jesus, but then denied him three times with curses. Despite his glaring weaknesses, you get the feeling from the gospel accounts that Jesus was fond of this rough-and-ready, uneducated fisherman. Peter was a constant, sometimes helpful companion in the crucial events of Jesus' life. After the threefold "Do you love me?" Jesus, now Risen Lord, says to Peter, "Feed my sheep" (John 21: 15–17). Acts of the Apostles tells the story of Peter's unique role in the early church as chief shepherd who cares for Christ's flock.

If Peter denied Christ three times with curses, Paul persecuted the Body of Christ with great zeal. Then one day on the road to Damascus, he heard those life-changing words "Saul, Saul, why do you persecute me?" When Paul asked for the identity of the voice, he heard, "I am Jesus whom you are persecuting." From that moment of faith's recognition, Paul completely identified with the person of Jesus and his apostolic mission for the salvation of the world.

The lasting significance of Peter and Paul is that they are witnesses to the Lord's resurrection. To believe that Jesus is truly risen and alive in us is possible only as a gift of the Holy Spirit (1 John 3: 24). The resurrection of Jesus, Saint Thomas Aquinas teaches us, is beyond the power of human reason to prove or to disprove. Human reason ("flesh and blood") at most can offer only arguments for or against the reality of the resurrection. Yet, our affirmation of faith is from the solid ground that human reason provides. The historical testimony of Peter and Paul supports our faith not only because they proclaimed the Lord's resurrection, but because they gave their lives in martyrdom. Today, we pray to share in the gift of Peter and Paul's faith, and promise—despite our own failings—to be witnesses to the Lord's resurrection by our good works of love.

Campion P. Gavaler, O.S.B.

Birth of John the Baptist, Cycle C
Luke 1: 57–66, 80

Gospel Summary

Luke introduces his gospel narrative of Jesus with the events surrounding the birth of John the Baptist. In prior verses related to our passage, we learn that a priest Zechariah and his wife Elizabeth have no children, both being well advanced in years. While Zechariah is performing his priestly duty in the sanctuary of the temple, an angel appears and says to him that Elizabeth will bear a son who was to be called John. But because Zechariah did not believe, and questioned the angel, he became unable to speak. After Elizabeth did give birth to a son, Zechariah wrote on a tablet, "John is his name." Immediately his tongue was freed and he spoke, blessing God. The child (whose name means "Yahweh has shown favor") grew and became strong in spirit, for he was to become a prophet of the Most High.

Life Implications

The unbreakable bond between the Jewish people and the people of the new covenant in God's plan of salvation is clearly evident in today's feast. It is from the Jewish people that John the Baptist, Mary, and Jesus are born so that the tender mercy of God will visit all people. It is from the Jewish people that the church receives the revelation of the most fundamental truths of faith. In the words of the Second Vatican Council, the church continues to draw "sustenance from the root of that well-cultivated olive tree onto which have been grafted the wild shoots, the Gentiles."

The most fundamental truth from which we draw sustenance is that God is present in human history as one who extends to us the favor of merciful love. We also learn from the Jewish people that the mystery of divine presence is beyond comprehension. The "I AM" of the divine name is a name beyond names (Exodus 3: 14 and John 8: 58). A child born of aged Abraham and Sarah or a bush that burns but is not consumed before Moses signals a presence beyond human understanding and control.

It is precisely because the mystery of the divine presence is beyond comprehension that the decision to trust or not to trust is inevitable for every one of us. Zechariah, upon hearing the outlandish words of the Lord's angel, did not trust and became mute, unable to speak a word (Luke 1: 20). Luke immediately afterward tells us that the Virgin Mary, too, was not able to understand the promise of the Lord's angel. However, her response "How can this be, since I have no relations with a man?" (Luke 1: 34) is asked out of trust, not out of doubt. The mystery even of human friendship can deal with a thousand difficulties and questions that are asked out of trust, but is deeply wounded by even one question asked out of doubt.

To receive the gift of recognizing the divine presence through faith calls forth a wholehearted response. The essence of that response is not only to trust, but also to bless God with praise and gratitude. When Zechariah wrote on the tablet "John is his name" immediately his mouth was opened and he spoke a blessing "because of the tender mercy of our God by which the daybreak from on high will visit us to shine on those who sit in darkness and death's shadow, to guide our feet into the path of peace" (Luke 1: 68–79). Mary's canticle of praise and gratitude in response to the favor of divine presence is one of the most beautiful blessings of the entire biblical tradition (Luke 1: 46–55).

Today's feast celebrating the birth of John the Baptist reminds us to pray again for the faith to recognize the divine presence in our lives, to trust in God's tender mercy with an undivided heart, and to bless God always and everywhere with a glad and grateful heart. Further, in the difficult circumstances that life brings to us all, only as a grateful expression of trust that God's will is to love us can we with confidence pray, "Thy will be done."

Campion P. Gavaler, O.S.B.

Assumption of the Blessed Virgin Mary
Luke 1: 39–56

Gospel Summary

Today's gospel offers us once again the beautiful story of Mary's visit to her cousin, Elizabeth, who is pregnant with John the Baptist. This act of thoughtful concern brings great joy to Elizabeth, sensed even by the child in her womb, but the highlight of the story is the hymn of praise and thanksgiving that Mary offers in her "Magnificat."

This splendid hymn transcends time and space as it sings of God's goodness and mercy to Mary and to all of us, in every place and at all times. In spite of the real and tragic presence of evil and sorrow in our world, the dark clouds of violence cannot hide the reality of God's love and concern for all the "lowly" ones. They have not been abandoned and their oppression at the hands of the "arrogant of mind and heart" will not last forever.

Life Implications

The victory that is celebrated in Mary's "Magnificat" is expressed in today's feast of the Assumption of Mary into heaven. Though the Scriptures do not explicitly refer to this event, it is implicit everywhere in the promise that God will "lift up" and give glory to all of us who, like Mary, trust in his goodness and obey his commandments.

The high and mighty ones of this world, who rely on power to serve their purposes, are inclined to ridicule those who accept the wisdom of Jesus and do their best to be a loving, caring presence in a much too violent world. Their way seems foolish and unpromising, but God is on their side and their ultimate victory is assured. Mary's glorious Assumption into heaven is celebrated, therefore, as the victory of love over hatred, of mercy over cruelty, and of gentleness over violence.

Unfortunately, in a society where sheer power is too often assumed to be the only means for getting things done, we are tempted to abandon the wisdom of Jesus. Indeed, we feel helpless in dealing with violence in our homes and in our streets. That is why this feast of the Assumption is so important, since it provides us with an opportunity to reaffirm our faith in God's promises. God really does remember his promises to Abraham and therefore to all of us believers, who are spiritual children of that great patriarch, whom Paul calls "the father of all of us" (Romans 4: 16). God really does intend to "lift up the lowly" and to "fill the hungry with good things." And if that is so, we should gladly sing with Mary, "My soul proclaims the greatness of the Lord; my spirit rejoices in God my Savior."

Demetrius R. Dumm, O.S.B.

Feast of All Saints
Matthew 5: 1–12a

Gospel Summary

For the feast of All Saints we are asked to reflect on the first, and perhaps most important, verses of Matthew's Sermon on the Mount. These verses have come to be called the Beatitudes. Since Matthew's Sermon on the Mount represents the moral ideals taught by Jesus, it is most appropriate to ponder their implications when we honor all the saints, that is, those who lived those ideals in an exemplary way.

The Beatitudes strike the keynote for all of the teaching that follows in the three lengthy chapters that make up the Sermon on the Mount. It is also true that the first Beatitude offers a key to the meaning of the seven remaining Beatitudes in Matthew's account.

The decisive word in this first Beatitude is the word "poor." Its meaning is derived from a Hebrew word meaning "an afflicted one." This name was applied to those Jews of the immediate pre-Christian era who were economically and politically powerless, but who continued to hope in God even though he seemed to have abandoned them. They were often poor in the sense of destitute, but their more basic poverty was in terms of power and control.

Jesus makes the daring statement that these downtrodden ones should in fact be declared blessed, that is, fortunate. What could possibly justify such a radical and apparently nonsensical conclusion? Jesus certainly does not intend to bless powerlessness as such. However, he does affirm the blessedness of those who, because they are powerless, are saved from the illusion that worldly power can in fact give us the only truly important and lasting gifts, such as, love, happiness, and life itself. Being delivered from that fateful illusion, they are free to turn to God, who is ready and willing to give them the Kingdom—something that earthly goods could never provide! It is therefore an attitude of humility and trust in the presence of God.

Life Implications

The ideal presented here must not be mistaken for a misguided passivity or timidity in the presence of the challenges of this life. Rather, it liberates us from self-centered and self-serving efforts, which will ultimately prove unproductive, so that we may be present to others in a loving, caring, and helpful way. This is summed up neatly in the seemingly paradoxical but very true statement, "The only gift we can keep is the one we give away!" Or, in gospel language, "What profit is there for one to gain the whole world and forfeit his life?" (Mark 8: 36)

The remaining seven Beatitudes are in a sense echoes of this primary one. Those who "mourn" are those who have dared to become vulnerable through loving. The "meek" have renounced power and violence as a means of acquiring happiness ... and thus find happiness! Those who "hunger and thirst for righteousness" have a passion for the reforms that will enable everyone to live and dream. Those who are "merciful" renounce anger and vengeance as they offer forgiveness. The "clean of heart" are the sincere and truthful ones who reject all that is mere sham and pretense in life.

The "peacemakers" promote forgiveness and reconciliation as the only sure way to peace. And those who are "persecuted" are those who persevere in the pursuit of these ideals in spite of ridicule from others who seem to be wise and prudent. Thus, the Beatitudes represent a radical but reliable program for true holiness ... as illustrated in the lives of that great army of saints whom we honor today.

Demetrius R. Dumm, O.S.B.

Dedication of the Lateran Basilica in Rome
John 2: 13–22

Gospel Summary

In order to celebrate the annual festival of Passover, Jesus goes up to Jerusalem. After he enters the temple area, he drives out those who are selling oxen, sheep, and doves, as well as the money changers, saying, "Stop making my Father's house a marketplace." When challenged to defend his outrageous action, Jesus replies, "Destroy this temple and in three days I will raise it up." His hearers think he is speaking of the temple in Jerusalem, which had been under construction for forty-six years. Only after Jesus rose from death did his disciples realize that he had spoken about the temple of his body.

Life Implications

The Basilica of Saint John Lateran in Rome symbolizes a crucial turning point in the long and remarkable history of the Catholic Church. The basilica was once a palace belonging to the Lateran family, dating back at least to the time of the persecution of Emperor Nero (A.D. 54–68). Emperor Constantine made a gift of the building to Pope Melchiade about the year 311. Before Constantine's rule, Christians were a persecuted sect struggling for survival within the hostile Roman Empire with its temples dedicated to the worship of many gods. The Lateran palace became the papal cathedral and the papal residence for more than a thousand years, despite being ravaged by the Vandals, by fires, and by earthquakes. Our parish churches may rightfully look to this cathedral church of the Bishop of Rome as their mother church. Its feast of dedication also may remind us of our spiritual bond with our brothers and sisters in many countries where Christians may not worship in public and are persecuted as an outlawed sect.

In today's gospel Jesus refers to the temple in Jerusalem as "my Father's house." That the invisible God manifests his presence in visible signs recognizable by faith is at the heart of biblical revelation. The opening hymn of Genesis celebrates the creation of the entire universe as the construction of a beautiful temple in which God dwells and may be glorified. God continues the revelation of divine presence not only in the universe and in the events of history, but in human structures—in the ark of the covenant leading the Jewish people through the wilderness, and in the temple Solomon built in Jerusalem.

In Jesus, revelation that God lives among us in visible signs reaches its climax. Jesus is the temple in which "the whole fullness of the deity dwells" (Colossians 2: 9). The theme of the divine presence in the universe, in the events of history, in human structures, and in Jesus is extended as in a rich tapestry even further. Jesus identifies his body with the new temple promised in messianic times, and in turn his body is identified with the Church and with each individual member of the Church. "Do you not know that you are the temple of God, and that the Spirit of God dwells in you" (1 Corinthians 3: 16, also read Ephesians 2: 19–22).

The Book of Revelation completes the theme of "temple and divine presence" to the fullest imaginable depth. In the end time of eternity, all earthly temples will be no more because God will be the temple. "I saw no temple in the city, for its temple is the Lord God almighty and the Lamb" (Revelation 21: 22). Now we are temples because God lives in us. Then, God will be the temple because we will live in him. Annie Dillard once remarked, "Home is the name of God." Because this is true, our faith can also help us have a new name for dying—Going Home.

Campion P. Gavaler, O.S.B.